THE
SCRABBLE®
BOOK

THE SCRABBLE® BOOK

Derryn Hinch

MASON / CHARTER

NEW YORK 1976

SCRABBLE® is the registered trademark of Selchow & Righter Co. Whenever used in the following text, it refers to the crossword game produced and marketed under the name Scrabble Crossword Game by Selchow & Righter under that trademark.

From *The Erection Set* by Mickey Spillane. Copyright © 1972 by Mickey Spillane. Reprinted by permission of the publishers, E. P. Dutton & Co., Inc.

Library of Congress Cataloging in Publication Data

Hinch, Derryn.
    The scrabble book.

    Includes index.
    1. Scrabble (Game) I. Title.
GV1507.S3H56   793.7'3   76-938
ISBN 0-88405-136-6
ISBN 0-88405-353-9 pbk.

For Eve
(even though her name is only worth
18 points on a triple-word square)

CONTENTS

ACKNOWLEDGMENTS

Thanks to the following people for their help in slaying the Jabberwock, for settling and sometimes inspiring Scrabble arguments, and for generally keeping my tiles straight in a manner that made this book possible:

My wife, Eve, for her nightly Scrabble games and for her marathon sessions immersed in dictionaries to help collate the diabolical lists of words used in this book.

My regular Scrabble opponents Leonora Burton and Anthony Burton; Nancy Davis, my editor—and my first southpaw Scrabble freak; Estelle Hoffman for her secretarial help.

The real Scrabble men, Alfred Butts and James Brunot, for their reminiscences and advice.

And my 86-year-old grandmother, Sarah Hinch, who was my first Scrabble opponent.

SOURCES

The following dictionaries were consulted as word
   authorities for this book:

Webster's Third New International Dictionary (unabridged), 1971 edition.

Funk & Wagnalls Standard College Dictionary, 1973 edition.

The Random House Dictionary of the English Language (unabridged
   edition), 1967.

scrabble (skrab'el) *V*. **-bled**, **-bling**. *v.i.* **1.** to scratch, scrape or paw, as with
the hands. **2.** To make irregular or meaningless marks; scribble. **3.** To
struggle or strive — *v.t.* **4.** To make meaningless marks on; scribble on. **5.**
To gather hurriedly; scrape together. — *n.* **1.** The act of scrabbling or
scrambling. **2.** A scrawling character mark, etc.; scribble. **3.** A sparse
growth, as of underbrush. **4.** The game of Scrabble.

—Funk & Wagnalls Standard College Dictionary

INTRODUCTION

Sophia Loren and Richard Burton did it to console him during one of his estrangements from Elizabeth Taylor.... Aging madam Lucy Longstreet did it in a Mickey Spillane bestseller to warn the hero that he was walking into a trap.... England's Queen Mother admitted, back in 1954, that she was a novice at it.... And out in Brooklyn, middle-aged widow Frances Koestler does it by herself to cure her insomnia....

The thing that Sophia and Richard and Lucy and the Queen Mother and Frances have in common is a passion—a passion for a game called Scrabble.

More than 25 years since the game came on the market and well over 40 years since it was invented by an out-of-work American architect during the Depression, Scrabble has established itself as the most successful word game in history. In fact, this game, originally called Criss-crosswords by its inventor, Alfred Butts, has been elevated through its style and stratagems, to the level of chess. These days anybody who used the words listed in a sample game in the lid of Scrabble kits would be annihilated. Words like *horn, farm, paste, mob*, and *bit* have been replaced by such demons as *haji, aalii, ilex, zloty*, and *zoa*.

Now there is offensive Scrabble, and defensive Scrabble, and blocks and bluffs, and razor-edged staredowns over challenged words that make poker hustlers look like George Washington when it comes to honesty. The newest rage is Tournament Scrabble—a highly competitive, stopwatch version of the game, in which players have a maximum of three minutes in which to complete a turn. There are also Mail Scrabble and Solitaire Scrabble.

Scrabble has been played on mountaintops and on safari in Africa. Nina Butts, wife of the inventor, tells a story of friends stumbling on a Scrabble game while on a tour of the Orient. "Part of the trip took them through Japan," she later told me. "They climbed one of the mountains. I don't think it was Fujiyama. Halfway up they saw two or three people resting by the side of the track. They were playing Scrabble."

As mentioned earlier, Mickey Spillane used the game to save the life of hero Dogeron Kelly, in his novel *The Erection Set*. Spillane's thrillers have sold more than 50 million copies, which just about matches the number of Scrabble sets in circulation.

If Scrabble buffs can get past the erotic picture of Spillane's naked wife on the cover and turn to page 269, they'll find Kelly about to walk into a killer's trap while former brothel-keeper Lucy Longstreet plays Solitaire Scrabble. As Spillane describes it:

> She was sitting by herself at a card table with a Scrabble game half-finished, an empty coffee cup beside her, looking as annoyed as hell.
>
> "Lose your partner?" I asked her.
>
> "Temporarily. Ain't much fun playing alone, so sit down, Johnny."
>
> She reached her leg out under the table and kicked the chair out for me, squinted at me impatiently and said, "Let me get this word down and you can play too."

(Kelly was obviously a hotshot Scrabble player.) There was something about her that wasn't hanging right, Spillane wrote, and when she picked up four tiles out of the holder and laid them down, it made a lousy job of Scrabble but a good piece of explanation. The word didn't fit, but it was clear enough. It spelled out T.R.A.P. (Kelly and Lucy Longstreet then hit the floor as the bullets started to fly, and Scrabble had saved a L.I.F.E.)

Frances Koestler of Brooklyn, who is now a Scrabble tournament player, says that Scrabble saved her life after her husband died six years ago. "We'd played Scrabble for years," she told me. "In fact, I was given one of the original sets of Criss-crosswords for a Christmas present back in 1943, and I've been playing ever since. Since my husband died, I've been an insomniac. But now I've learned to play Solitaire Scrabble. At night when I can't sleep, instead of having a beer, I'll play Solitaire for a couple of hours, and, do you know, I've trained myself not to let either hand cheat."

Back during the Scrabble craze days of the 1950s it was considered very avant-garde to play "smutty Scrabble" with four-letter words at Hollywood parties—before the words were diverted to the screen. And when Queen Elizabeth, the Queen Mother, visited New York in 1954, *The New York Times* saw fit to print the fact that she bought a deluxe Scrabble set, complete with a revolving turntable, from F. A. O. Schwarz.

Despite such royal interest, one of the major appeals of this game of mental gymnastics is that it is a game for everyone. For example, when the first American Scrabble tournaments were organized in late 1973 and early 1974, the grid board with its 225 squares produced winners from all sorts of backgrounds and occupations. In the Baltimore finals a truckdriver was the winner, a parole officer was second, a professional army man was third, a student, fourth, and a sanitation worker, fifth. The truckdriver successfully defended his title the following year.

In New York they had people ranging in age from 16 to 84 flocking to the Brooklyn War Memorial each Sunday where 2,000 contestants were whittled down to 50 finalists. Selchow & Righter, the company that now owns and manufactures Scrabble, hired a film crew to make a Scrabble documentary, and chesty young women paraded around in T-shirts that spelled out S.C.R.A.B.B.L.E. P.L.A.Y.E.R.S. in game tiles on the front and that were so tight that the *B* tiles looked as though they should have been worth more than the legal three points.

Swept up in the new Scrabble-mania, four students in Lakewood, California, set a world Scrabble marathon record of 100 hours that gained recognition in the *Guinness Book of World Records.* Their record held for just over two years until in August 1975, four "down under" Scrabble fanatics in Sydney, Australia, played non-stop in a shop window for 120 hours.

With Scrabble now in the big league, it's time for a complete book on the game, covering its history, strategy, and aberrations. There are sections on how to play for fun, how to play for blood, how to score "bingos," those lucrative seven-letter words that include a 50-point bonus, and how to improve your strategic vocabulary so that you always score between 400 and 600 points in a game. There are also chapters on Tournament Scrabble and variations on the game, such as Ecology Scrabble—in which various letters, usually the blanks, are recycled during the game—and Unscrabble, which you play in reverse.

This book tells Scrabble freaks as well as Scrabble novices "everything you always wanted to know about Scrabble but didn't have the tiles to ask." For example, did you know that there are 69 two-letter words that are acceptable (according to Funk & Wagnalls) and that some tournament players have memorized every one of them? They include good blocking words like *xi* and *ka* and excellent hook-words like *aa* and *ut* and *ai*.

It will no doubt come as welcome news to many Scrabble players that they are in good company if they hate to lose. I do. According to actor Richard Burton, the voluptuous actress Sophia Loren is a good Scrabble player but she detests losing. "She's stupendously intelligent," Burton said, after one game with the sultry Italian film star, "but she can't bear to lose. You know she beat me twice ... in English yet."

So this is the game of Scrabble—played by widows alone and by film stars, jet-setters, truckdrivers, royalty, hustlers, writers, and indefatigable students. Dustin Hoffman plays it, and so does Russian novelist Vladimir Nabokov. So did Prime Minister Nehru of India and Oscar Hammerstein II. Madame Giscard d'Estaing, wife of the French president, plays it in French and in English and consistently wins in both languages.

I hope the following chapters will improve your Scrabble and settle the inevitable arguments that erupt around Scrabble tables everywhere.

I should point out that *scrabble* is a playable word, meaning "to scratch, scrape or paw with the hands." If you play it right and somehow stretch it through two triple-word squares, it can be worth 203 points.

A word of warning though: the word *scrabble* also means "to make irregular or meaningless marks."

Ah, I know the feeling well. . . .

Part I

THE HISTORY OF SCRABBLE

1 THE MAN WHO INVENTED SCRABBLE

IN THE EARLY DAYS I WAS INTRODUCED TO A WOMAN
AS THE INVENTOR OF SCRABBLE. AND SHE SAID "OH,
IS THAT SO? MY HUSBAND JUST LOVES IT. I WISH
YOU'D TELL ME HOW TO COOK IT."
                    —*Alfred Mosher Butts, 1975*

Few people nowadays are likely to confuse Scrabble, the world's most popular word game, with that Pennsylvania dish of fried pork scraps and meal called scrapple. There is a vague connection. The food scrap days of the Depression inspired the unemployed Butts to come up with an adult game which he hoped would make him rich. "If there hadn't been any Depression in the thirties," Butts said, "there wouldn't have been any Scrabble, I don't think."

Butts was an out-of-work architect living in Jackson Heights, Queens, New York, at the time. He was 34 years old, married, and, apart from his then unneeded talents as a designer, he had a passion for mind games. It was an interest shared in his youth with four older brothers, and it grew from anagrams and cards to crosswords and cryptograms and finally in 1933 developed into a vague game idea he called "It." Later he would call it Criss-crosswords, and still later it would become the game known internationally as Scrabble.

"Although the Depression started in 1929, my job as an architect held up for a couple more years," Butts recalled. "Then there was no architectural work, and I decided I'd try to think of something else to do."

Butts discovered a phenomenon in that Depression that repeated itself during the 1974–75 recession: when times are hard, with unemployment lines long and luxuries out of reach, people turn to escapist forms of entertainment. They read more books, they go to movies, and they play more games.

"It seemed to me that entertaining people was more lucrative than trying to do something for people," Butts said. "I remember, and this is

3

going back 40 years mind you, that radio was a big thing then. Everybody had a radio and actors were big ... so were athletes and authors. Well, I couldn't do anything like that; so I thought 'I'll try to build a game, an adult game.'"

Butts, who had an architect's analytical mind, looked around at existing games on the market and analyzed them. There were numbers games that used dice and cards, like bingo, and there were board games with men to be moved, like checkers and chess. All of them seemed to be old.

"Putting men on a board started with checkers and finally led up to chess," Butts said, "and the numbers games started with dice. I believe the Egyptians had dice. Of course, in cards there was also bridge. It was still being improved in those days. There was bridge and auction bridge, and contract bridge was just coming out. Now, when you say 'bridge,' there is just one game. But most of them were really old games. Mah-Jongg was just an old Chinese game updated, and Backgammon was having a comeback such as it had again in 1975. But Backgammon was a combination of men on a board like checkers and the luck of a dice throw."

Butts looked around and discovered that the other category of game was the word game. "Playing with letters seemed to be the only other possibility, and there didn't seem to be anything but anagrams available." Architect Butts decided that would be the game upon which he would try to improve.

He credits his family background for having a lot to do with that decision. "You know we had this old family homestead in Poughkeepsie, New York. A lot of articles say that I was an out-of-work Poughkeepsie architect when I invented Scrabble. That wasn't true. I was born there and lived there as a child, but I was married and living in New York when Scrabble came along."

Whatever Butts says, though, the seeds for the game that would become Scrabble were sown at Poughkeepsie. As he recalled, "The five of us boys would play all these games. Anagrams was a popular one. The trouble was we'd keep using the same little words over and over again."

Butts's older brother, Allison, who later became a professor of metallurgy at Lehigh University, decided the game needed beefing up. "He got a book, and every time we used a word we had to write it in the book and then you weren't allowed to use it again," Butts remembered. "We built up quite a book with all these words in it. It forced us to use different words all the time and, looking back on it, it helped build our vocabulary."

Later the Butts brothers found a spare letter from another anagram set and decided to add that to the game and use it as a wild card. Years later that principle would foster the blank tiles in Scrabble. "We drew the letters out of a bag and used the extra one as a wild card and tried to make anagrams. I won't say that was the beginning of Scrabble ... but it was something that led into it."

□

In 1933, when he was searching for a game idea and thinking back to his childhood word games, Butts decided the big problem with anagrams was that each set was "just a jumble of letters." He said, "I still wasn't sure what sort of game would turn out, but I knew I had to work out some fair distribution of the letters ... the way you would normally use them in words. That idea also came to me from cryptograms. I was very interested in them and in crossword puzzles, too."

The code aficionado recalled how he had always been impressed by an Edgar Allan Poe mystery called "The Gold Bug" in which the case was solved when the protagonist realized that *e* was the most frequently used letter in the alphabet and therefore held the key to deciphering cryptograms.

The fledgling inventor soon discovered, however, that there was a flaw in using cryptograms as a guideline for his letters. "I discovered cryptograms gave false importance to some letters. Like the word *the* appears often in a coded message, and that means the letter *h* is used abnormally." As a double check, Butts tore pages out of the daily newspapers and laboriously tabulated the usage of all letters on endless charts and graphs.

The formula he came up with was that in 100 letters there should be a maximum of 12 tiles with the letter *e*; nine for the *i* and in decreasing numbers for other letters, down to one each for the *z*, *q*, *x*, and *j*.

Now he had the letters, but Alfred Butts still didn't have a game—except for a sort of deluxe anagram set. "The next thing I decided was that each person would draw seven letters and try to make a seven-letter word on the table. If he couldn't, then the first player would draw another letter and try to put that in his word. He was only allowed to keep seven letters in his hand, so he would have to discard one, and the following player would have the choice of picking up that discard or drawing a fresh letter from the bag."

(The way Butts described that game to me, it sounded suspiciously like an alphabet version of the well-known card game called knock poker.)

The players kept drawing and discarding letters until one of them could make a seven-letter word. He put the word down and was declared the winner of that hand. "My wife Nina was the guinea pig," Butts said. "I tried out all the ideas on her."

The next step in the evolution of Scrabble came when Butts realized there was no reward for a player who made his or her seven-letter word out of the more difficult letters in the alphabet. "I thought, well, some of these letters are only here once, and you ought to get something more for them. So I thought, why not put a score on each of the letters. Then we can add up each letter and give each word a score. Suddenly, I realized that by doing that each hand didn't have to be a complete game. If a person went out with a complete seven-letter word, the others could then try to make the best possible word in their hand with six or five or four letters, and they could count that score up too."

Butts thought he had "something pretty good." He decided to make up some sets of letters and test them on his friends, and he gave the game a name: Lexiko. "That was where my architectural training came in handy under the circumstances. I realized I could make these things up by drawing a block of letters, getting it blueprinted and then putting the blueprint on a sheet of plywood. When it dried, I could saw it up and make a set of letters."

Butts apparently decided on limiting his number of letter tiles to 100 because that was all he thought he'd have the patience to cut out with his fretsaw. "The beauty of this, and remember it was during the Depression, was that I didn't have to spend a lot of money to get somebody else to make up a set of letters. I could do it all myself."

To complete the test-model games, Butts decided he needed racks for each player to store his word-in-the-making. "I couldn't afford much, and this is funny, so I went down to the local lumber yard. I'd got the idea for racks from the Mah-Jongg tile holders. Down at the lumber yard I found something that was perfect—a piece of ordinary molding like the stuff that goes around the ceiling or the baseboard of a room. I bought it in big lengths and chopped it down to the size I wanted.

"And you know something? When Scrabble became big business and they could have made a die in any shape they wanted, they still kept the same old shape for the racks. Sometimes I stained it to dress it up a bit, but it was just a piece of old molding."

Butts's guinea pig friends liked his game, and, full of enthusiasm, he sent it off to the game manufacturers. None of them were the slightest bit interested. "The game came back with nothing. No suggestions for improvement . . . nothing. There were two big companies then, Parker Brothers, who made Monopoly, and Milton Bradley. I know I sent it to them and to some others, but I don't know if I sent it to Selchow & Righter."

The inventor still believed in his game. "I never lost faith in it. I knew there were the makings of something good there. I thought, okay, the game companies don't like it as it is. I'll improve it."

Butts then came up with what he thought was the clincher: he decided his new game, still called "It," should be played on a board. "I thought, let's play it on a board, like a crossword puzzle. So I put the letters on a board and moved them around a bit, and I don't know how the inspiration came to me, but then I decided to put premium squares on the board, the double-letter scores and the triple-word scores. I knew this was what I wanted. You see, I had been trying to get something that would be a good balance between luck and skill. By putting scores on the letters and then putting in premium squares, I had it. There was luck if you drew a high letter, but it was skill if you could get that letter in the proper place on the board. Those two things made a very good balance. Now I really had something. I could see it. And, again, I could make it myself."

Butts drew his game board with its special squares, made blueprints of it, and then went to the local dime store and bought ordinary checkerboards, on which he pasted his layouts. Then he went back to the game companies. All of them, including Selchow & Righter, rejected the game again. Most thought the game was "too highbrow" or "too serious" or "too complicated."

The manufacturers who rejected the game then now rank alongside the film companies who thought *Gone With The Wind* was too long to be a commercial success. Said Butts, "Not one of them sent back a nice letter saying, 'This is an interesting game, but why don't you do such-and-such.' The game companies were only interested in what I'd call childish things. They wanted games where you had a spinner that said something, and then you moved a man on the board. That sort of thing. They wanted games that sold at Christmas time, and that was the end of it. Next Christmas they'd come up with another game for children."

Alfred and Nina Butts had no children and were staunch believers that there was nothing wrong with a game for adults. Mrs. Butts said, "Everybody says games have to be for children and that games for adults are wrong. Well we didn't want this to be turned into a game for children."

The dogged development of the game and the repeated rejections from the manufacturers lasted from 1933 to 1938.

"Although everybody turned me down, my friends still liked the game, and occasionally I'd make up sets for them, and they'd give them to other friends. I had an electric jigsaw, and I used to use it in our apartment to cut out the tiles. My wife thought the neighbors would think we were terrible ... the noise I made. I didn't make many sets, though—I guess about 50."

People who got near those 50 sets loved the game, and several approaches were made to Butts for him to manufacture the sets himself and other people would market them. He turned them down. "This was something people didn't understand. I never had any intention of manufacturing the game. My idea all along was to invent a successful game and then turn it over to some company and get a royalty. I kept thinking about authors who wrote a book and then collected a royalty while somebody else sold it. I remember one fellow who wanted to sell it for me. He owned a store and kept pleading with me to make up some games for him to sell, but I wasn't interested.

"Another man was all set to take the game over, and he wrote out a contract, and he was going to pay me, based on the retail value of the sets, a colossal royalty. He went to Macy's, and he was going to sell it to them and they told him to make a few changes in it, and they'd consider it. But that fell through."

Butts said one of the reasons he wasn't interested in physically making a lot of sets and setting up a business was that he was an architect, and architecture was his "whole drive" in life. "With the Depression over, I was getting back into architecture. I wasn't interested in spending all my time making sets. I'd make up a set or two now and again and Criss-crosswords became a game that my wife and I played occasionally with friends," he said.

Butts was rehired as an architect in 1939, but his first post-Depression job was with the Emergency Relief Bureau of New York. "I was a statistician. I'd never studied statistics; so that didn't go on for very long." It did go on long enough for him to meet, and become friends with, another man in the social services field, a government social worker named Jim Brunot. Butts introduced Brunot to his homemade game and gave a set of Criss-crosswords to Brunot and his wife, Helen. This was just before World War II, and Butts was at the end of another round of rejections from the game manufacturers.

Then, as the inventor of Scrabble puts it, his game "lay fallow for a while" through the war years of the early forties, until in 1947 he was contacted by Brunot, who was just back from a stint in Washington, where he had served as the wartime executive director of the President's War Relief and Control Board. Brunot put a proposition to Butts, resurrected his game, changed the name of Criss-crosswords to Scrabble, and launched a phenomenon that *Look* magazine called "the new parlormania."

Alfred Butts, with his trusty jigsaw had made 50 sets of his much-spurned game. Brunot would generate a business that produced more than 50 million sets of Scrabble in a word game explosion that led *Life* magazine to comment in 1953, "No game in the history of the trade has ever sold so rapidly."

2 SCRABBLE HITS A GUSHER

I'M LOOKING FOR A QUIET LITTLE BUSINESS IN THE
COUNTRY."

—*James Brunot, 1947*

It was the summer of 1952, and Jim Brunot and his wife, Helen, were in bluegrass country down in Kentucky. That state may be renowned for its race horses, but it also has a lot of pedigreed sheep, and the Brunots were looking for a new breeding ram to take back to their 200-head flock on their 100-acre farm in Connecticut, about 75 miles north of New York City.

Brunot was thinking of sheep and stud farming and not thinking kindly, if at all, about the game of Scrabble, which he had bought from Alfred Butts four years previously and which had only one thing in common with sheep farming: it was fleecing him.

The game that he had acquired from Butts and rechristened Scrabble was forcing him to scrabble about for more cash to keep afloat his small, but impressive-sounding Production & Marketing Company, which he was operating out of a tiny, disused schoolhouse in Dodgingtown, Connecticut. He had lost money in his first year of production, and the next, and the next, and was losing money in the fourth and probably final year.

Brunot's partner, a man named Lester Twitchell, had already dropped out, and in Brunot's mind his most sound business decision had been not to quit his job in New York while trying to get Scrabble off the ground. "I was earning a pretty good salary for those days," he recalled, "and fortunately I had a little bit of a nest egg that I could get to once in a while. We weren't even breaking even, although I was confident that if we could just hold on, it would pay off. Whether or not we could hold on though was another story."

☐

In 1949, the first year of production for Scrabble, he had sold 2,251 sets and lost $450. In 1950 sales had increased to 4,800 sets and had jumped again to 8,500 in 1951. The sales graph was showing an upswing each year, but production was expensive: the boards were made in New York, the tiles in New Jersey, and the packaging was completed in Connecticut. So in the middle of his fourth year as a businessman, Jim Brunot was still bathing in red ink.

□

The Brunots returned from their successful sheep-shopping vacation, expecting to find orders for about 200 sets. Instead of 200 requests, Brunot discovered that during his weeklong absence 2,500 orders had poured in. That was more than he had sold in his entire first year of production. "At first, I thought it was a mistake," he said. "Then I thought—and this persisted even when Scrabble became a craze—that it was just a flash in the pan."

The following week Brunot's protesting mailman delivered letters demanding 3,000 Scrabble sets, and the week after that the avalanche of order form continued. Jim Brunot had hit a gusher—nearly 20 years after inventor Alfred Butts had tried to escape the Depression by playing around with an idea for a revolutionary word game.

Brunot's rented one-room schoolhouse and his own home and garage were awash with Scrabble boxes, tiles, boards, and a mountain of orders for his game. By the end of that year the frazzled Scrabble man had sold nearly 60,000 sets and had quit his job in New York to try to handle a business that was becoming more chaotic, albeit more lucrative, every day.

His factory got bigger—he moved into a woodworking plant in nearby Bethel, Connecticut—and his staff was increased from two to more than 30, and they worked day shifts and night shifts. "It was like pouring the sets into a bottomless pit," Brunot said. "We had people working all day and others all night, and still we were thousands and thousands of orders behind . . . it was unbelievable. At one stage we had a backlog of 60,000 orders."

By 1954 Brunot's Production & Marketing Company had sold four and a half million sets of this game called Scrabble.

America was deep in a Scrabble craze. Brunot and Butts had their photographs in *Look* magazine as they happily cavorted around a giant Scrabble board specially made for the occasion, and they were written up in *Life* and *Reader's Digest*. Shops whose toy and game buyers managed to snare a few sets plastered "We Have Scrabble" signs in their windows, and the game even became a cartoon topic in magazines like *The New Yorker*. One cartoon showed a jilted bride left at the altar as the groom sprinted from the church. The best man was lamely explaining to the tearful girl, "He's just heard they've got a new supply of Scrabble at Macy's." Another showed a portly executive, on vacation on Long Island with his wife, standing on the end of a jetty and glowering at a looming bank of storm clouds. Said the wife, "Oh dear, another Scrabble day."

An article of the day in *Life* magazine noted: "In intellectual circles the game is played in French and Latin; in Hollywood games of dirty Scrabble are in constant progress; in New York the guys-and-dolls set has converted Scrabble into the hottest gambling game since gin rummy." *Life* said there seemed to be no limit to the number of Scrabble players, "which may finally include everyone old enough to spell and still not too feeble to lift the tiles." The boom in the game's nationwide popularity was so unexpected, yet so intense and unflagging, that Marvin Kaye, in his book *A Toy Is Born*, described Scrabble as "one of the great unsolved mysteries of the American game business."

□

Why did it take off? What suddenly triggered a stampede for a game that Alfred Butts had been unsuccessfully hawking around for nearly 20 years? A game that Brunot himself admitted to me he had always regarded as a sport "for the egghead constituency"?

I had heard what I thought was an apocryphal story about some New York department store executive playing Scrabble at a summer resort in the Catskills, then returning to New York to discover that his own firm did not stock this new "in" game. "The story is absolutely true," Jim Brunot said, "but it wasn't in the Catskills . . . I believe it was on Long Island. The man involved was Jack Straus, the chairman of the board of Macy's at that time. He'd apparently played the game with friends during the summer out on the island, and when he got back to town, he called up his game department and asked them to send up a few sets to his office. It sent them all into a panic. They didn't stock Scrabble. Somebody had heard of the game—well, they ought to have because we'd been trying to sell it to them for ages—but they couldn't remember who, or where, we were.

"Somebody in the toy or game department remembered that we'd been trying to sell Scrabble to them on the grounds that it was doing so well at Marshall Field's in Chicago. So finally they called Marshall Field's and tracked us down to Newtown, Connecticut. There was a great flurry of excitement. I think we got calls from three different departments. Anyway, Mr. Straus finally got his Scrabble set, and we got a big order from Macy's."

Brunot still chuckles when he tells that story and others about the fluke birth of Scrabble. The man who ultimately made more than several million dollars out of Scrabble relishes anecdotes about his game-child.

James Brunot, an affable fellow in his seventies, who looks like he could be Arthur Godfrey's brother, has often been described as a "social worker" who bought Scrabble from Butts because he was about to retire and wanted some little thing to amuse him at his home in the country. He has also been described in the past as a close friend of Butts. In fact, they were more acquaintances than friends, and circumstances more than a kinship threaded their lives together. To call Brunot a "social worker" is about the same as calling Dick Tracy a rookie cop or Jack Nicklaus a weekend golfer. And as for retiring, Brunot says, "I wasn't about to retire . . . I was only 44 then."

□

Jim Brunot's winding path to a game that would ultimately make him a millionaire with a house and farm in Connecticut and a vacation villa on millionaire's row at Hilton Head Island in South Carolina, started out in Pennsylvania. "I was born in Greensburg, in western Pennsylvania, but my father died when I was an infant, and my mother remarried a man from Hammond, Indiana; so I spent my childhood in the Midwest."

Brunot then went to the University of Chicago, where he formed a college friendship with Lester Twitchell, who, for a short time, would be his partner in the Scrabble business. After he completed college, Brunot went straight into social work administration, and in 1938 he took a job in New York as head of a welfare department in an organization called the State Charities' Aid Association. This was about the same time that Alfred Butts was coming to the end of years of heartbreaking disappointment trying to get game manufacturers like Parker Brothers and department stores like Macy's interested in his game of Criss-crosswords.

Brunot recalled: "Our offices were down on Twenty-second Street and Fourth Avenue, and I remember Alfred Butts was employed at the time at the Russell Sage Foundation, which was also a social services organization. Their offices were right across the street from ours, and there was a great deal of interchange between the two organizations. Butts and his wife and my wife and I were in the same circle of friends, and it was through this that I got to know about the game of Criss-crosswords that Butts had invented."

□

In 1940 Brunot went down to Washington "supposedly on loan for a few months" and became involved in several federal projects. First he worked for an emergency organization in the Social Security Agency, known as the Office of Community Defense Services, and then became director of the President's War Relief and Control Board. His "few months" stretched into six years, and it was during that time that Brunot and his wife became real enthusiasts for the homemade Criss-crosswords game. They were still playing in 1946 when Brunot returned to New York to run the budget committee for the national organization of the Community Chest.

"My wife and I had our place in Connecticut then, and although I wasn't interested in retiring, I *was* interested in having something to do other than a salaried job," he said. "I thought it would be nice to start a little niche of some sort. I certainly didn't have the idea of starting something so important to me that I would be completely dependent on it."

The person who suggested to Brunot that Scrabble could be just the "little niche" he was looking for was a woman called Neva Deardorff—a New York social worker who probably ranks as the world's first Scrabble fanatic. She was a friend of both Brunot and Butts and, in fact, introduced them to each other. Neva had been a booster of Butts's Criss-crosswords since the mid-thirties, and, as Butts recalled it, "she was always after me to have more sets made up."

In 1942, through Neva Deardorff, there was a fledgling marketing attempt by a man called Chester Ives in Danbury, Connecticut. (On one of the old blueprint style boards that Butts gave me is the inscription: "Chester B. Ives, Distributor, 1 Library Place, Danbury, Conn. Copyright 1942 by C.B.I." Down one side of the board is the wording "Originated by Alfred M. Butts.")

Butts said, "I made up some sets for him and he sold them in his bookstore in Danbury. Then I told him he'd have to make the sets himself. He made some, but he ran into trouble getting a copyright for the board, and we abandoned it after making only a few sets."

Four years after that, at Neva Deardorff's instigation, Brunot and Twitchell decided to give Scrabble a go. "I forget when we started," Brunot said. "It was 1946 or 1947, but we formed a company, and it sounded grand. 'The Production & Marketing Company.' Actually, we started out on a very small scale. We had very little capital . . . just a couple of thousand dollars."

They wrote Butts a letter, offering him a royalty if he would let them take over Criss-crosswords and try to make a commercial success of the game. By this time, you get the impression that Alfred Butts, now back into architecture, thought the whole thing was a pipe dream. So many schemes to market his game had almost worked. For example, after the Danbury bookstore incident, Butts and Ives's wife (Chester Ives was then away in the army) had had a promising business deal outlined to them by a man named Herbert Simonds. "He was a consulting engineer with offices on Fifth Avenue. He talked big money, and he was going to give us good royalties—up to 20 percent of the retail price of each set." That project, like all the others, faltered when the game was offered to department store game buyers and they rejected it with the now familiar plaint that it was "too slow ... too professional-looking ... not glamorous enough."

The next time though it was different: Brunot, Twitchell, and Butts made a royalty agreement based on the chatty, personal letter approach from the two would-be marketers. In later years when either side showed the letter to a lawyer, the response was always the same. The attorneys all wondered how they could set up a business deal on what amounted to a gentlemen's handshake agreement.

In the letter Brunot spelled out his fears about competition if the game succeeded and worried about the chance that somebody else would steal their idea. The letter said in part: "Despite the costly problems, we will be glad to pay you from time to time for the next two years a fee equal to 5 percent of the net wholesale selling price."

The deal was made, and for more than 20 years the letter held up as a binding agreement between the inventor and the new owner.

Butts's wife, Nina, said later, "Jim Brunot was a wonderful man to us. Alfred was absolutely lucky to come across a man like that. Just think how many people would have taken advantage of that letter and shoved him right out. But Brunot never did." Not only did Brunot *not* shove Butts out, but over the years he paid him royalties of more than one million dollars for the game Butts had invented over breakfast one morning in the Depression.

Once Brunot had the rights to the game, he moved to make sure he had them all. He knew about Simonds, and in July 1947 Butts handed him a letter from Simonds in which Simonds stated flatly, "I have relinquished any formal interest I may have had [in the game] and hope to benefit indirectly."

Finally, Brunot got a copyright on the unique game board and was ready to go into business. Ironically, his main goal was to do what Butts had tried to do previously. "I wanted to get the game into reasonably attractive shape, package it well, and get the rules worked out so they were clear and concise. Then I thought we'd try to turn it over to one of the game manufacturers and try to work out an arrangement for some sort of royalty."

Like Butts, Brunot went around to the manufacturers and the big department stores, trying to sell the game. And, like Butts, he received a cold response. "They told me it was too complicated, too slow and 'uninteresting pictorially,' whatever that meant," Brunot said.

He decided to go it alone, and his first shipment went out in December 1948. Before that he had to come up with a name. His lawyers had decided that Criss-crosswords was too close to being a generic name and, being descriptive, could not be registered as a trademark. "We submitted quite a long list of names," Brunot said. "I wish I'd kept it. I can't remember what all of them were, but I know one of them was Logo-loco."

Who came up with the suggestion *Scrabble*?

"You know I can't for the life of me remember. We've tried for years to remember how it came up, and we couldn't. It was just one of this long list that we submitted to our patent lawyer. We had another name, our favorite—and I can't now remember it either—but the lawyers said it was too close to another name already on the market. So we had to drop it, and Scrabble was the one we ended up with."

□

The game, which has now sold more than 50 million sets, was started with an initial run of 1,000 sets.

"Why didn't we make more? Because, frankly, it was all we cared to afford at that time. Of that first thousand, we only sold about three or four dozen. We sent 200 sets, or 250, to people who had known the original Butts game and to our circle of friends at Russell Sage, etc. And we sent some to people we'd played Criss-Crosswords with in Washington during the war. We also sent sets to friends of ours and acquaintances whom we thought, quite frankly, as being a sort of 'egghead constituency.' We sent them as gifts, but we enclosed mail order forms for additional sets. That form of soliciting, putting order forms in the sets we sold, accounted for nearly all our business until 1952."

In those days Brunot and his wife could have stared down the best mail-order man in the business. They'd send out the sets, free of charge, to friends and acquaintances. Then they'd follow up with a form letter that said: "Recently we shipped you a game of Scrabble. We hope you enjoyed it. This is a new type of game, etc., etc., which is not widely distributed. If you know of any friends who might be interested, please send us their name and address on the enclosed postcard."

Reminiscing in retirement, Brunot said, "We got hundreds of replies. We took all the names from the postcards and sent the people circulars saying that 'so and so' told us you might be interested in buying a game of Scrabble. We used that tactic until 1952, when we didn't need it any more. By then we couldn't keep up with the demand."

Back in 1948–49 there was scant demand to keep up with. At the end of the first year, the Production & Marketing Company had sold 2,251 sets and had lost $450. "We were still in the stage of having to support the company," Brunot said, "rather than having the company support us. That first year it became a little difficult for Twitchell, who had worked at Marshall Field's and who had since retired, to keep it going on his retirement benefits. Actually, it became a little burdensome for me too." Twitchell was bought out and he retired to Chicago, where he continued for a while to be Brunot's sales representative in the Midwest.

Scrabble continued to lose money. Brunot maintained his job in New York City, and Mrs. Brunot started to have more faith in her sheep than in the word game. Then came the trip to Kentucky to check out the pedigreed ram and, as Brunot put it, "when we got home, the place was in chaos. The two people we had working for us at that time were completely snowed under with inquiries and orders."

Brunot held on to his job in the city until the end of 1952 because "I wasn't sure that this wasn't just a flash in the pan. Neither was anyone else who was connected with it. I wasn't sure that it wouldn't just collapse just as quickly as it started. Therefore, what we did was just hang on from month to month without too much planning."

This casual approach to the business was what started such rumors as the one that Scrabble sets were all made by hand by two "eccentric old men in the mountains" who weren't interested in money.

□

One thing that Brunot did not expect was the onslaught of toy and game jobbers who descended on his quiet schoolhouse-cum-factory. "We'd had no experiences with jobbers," he said. "I was amazed at some of the tactics they used. One fellow came up to our factory with I don't know how many thousands of dollars—in cash—that he said he would pay us that day for our entire factory output. The idea was that he would pay us for every set in the place and he would have exclusive control over distribution to retailers."

One visitor, who was spurned by Brunot when he tried to place a large order at the deluged factory, noticed a stack of cartons in the building. Each carton had the name *Selchow & Righter* stamped on it. The buyer hotfooted it down to Selchow & Righter and cornered their sales vice-president and said, "I know you've got something to do with this crazy new game because I've been up there to Connecticut, and I've seen your cartons all over the place."

"The sales rep at S & R, a Mr. Anderson it was," Brunot recalled, "told the man quite truthfully that he had no idea what he was talking about." What had happened, according to Brunot, was that when he was assembling the games, he had gone to several game manufacturers for parts. "We weren't making the games ourselves, except for cutting up the moldings into racks on a saw in my garage. We were just assembling them. As I said, we had the boxes made in one place and the tiles, made of plywood in those days, made in New Jersey, and we had the letters printed on a laminated sheet and had them cut up and stuck on the ply."

The boards, as it turned out, were being made by none other than Selchow & Righter—makers of Parcheesi boards for more than 70 years. Apparently, the factory hadn't told the sales people of the arrangement.

"It caused quite a stir," Brunot remembered. "I don't know what went on at the other end, but they called me and said they were going to cut off our supply of boards immediately." It was, as Brunot recalled it, "a hot time" for a few days, and he did manage to find an alternative supplier who could have, at short notice, made up the boards "even though the quality might not have been as good." But the people at Selchow & Righter, a firm that had twice rejected Scrabble, now had evidence in its own books of Scrabble's burgeoning success. "As it turned out," Brunot explained, "they knew as much about our sales figures and what was happening to it in popularity as we did. After all, they were supplying the boards. It was then we started discussing the possibility of them taking over."

Brunot's Production & Marketing Company and Selchow & Righter ironed out a "manufacturing and marketing agreement" that took effect in 1953. Under the agreement the big game company earned the right to manufacture, exclusively, the standard Scrabble set in its trademarked plum-colored box. "We retained the right to manufacture anything except the standard set. We could still make the deluxe sets, the foreign sets. We retained those rights. And it worked out very happily all round."

In 1971 James Brunot sold outright all trademarks, copyrights, and claims for his Scrabble name in the United States and Canada to Selchow & Righter, with final payments over five years to end in 1976. At the same time he sold complete Australian rights to T. R. Urban & Co. and British and other rights to J. W. Spear & Sons Ltd.

Why did he sell out, and why, especially, did he take the first big step of letting Selchow & Righter into the act back in 1953? "Well," he said, "there were two major considerations. One was that the whole thing was getting too big for us. I've said before I wanted a quiet little business in the country. The game was suddenly so popular it was becoming a monster."

Brunot said it had become a "nightmare." "We were working 24 hours a day and producing only about 5,000 sets a week. Within two weeks of our working out this arrangement with Selchow & Righter, we increase that to 15,000 sets a week. Production jumped more than 200 percent per week."

The other factor was that Brunot and his staff were getting bogged down in paper work and politics. "We had no real sales organization, and we got into some awful wrangles with big stores. We had some so-called 'manufacturers representatives,' but we were relatively small. In our innocence we made no differentiation between the adult game department and the toy department or whatever, and it caused a lot of squabbles. I remember we got into a great mess with Marshall Field's. We had to either get our own line of games, a complete line apart from Scrabble and build up a sales force, or let somebody else with the organization and know-how handle it. Making a deal with Selchow & Righter seemed to me to be the logical thing to do."

Another factor, Brunot admits, was that he still had a feeling of uncertainty over how long the game could remain popular. "One of the things that was always in the back of my mind was that it would turn out to be a short-lived craze."

By 1971, when Jim Brunot decided to sell everything to Selchow & Righter, no strings attached, it was obvious though that his doubts about Scrabble being a short-lived craze were unfounded. Admittedly, there was a slight drop-off in sales in 1956, but, says Brunot, "it has been building up ever since that time. There has been no year since when the sales haven't gone up." Selchow & Righter are selling more than one million Scrabble sets a year, according to Brunot, "and I now believe that Scrabble is here to stay. I sold the whole thing because, frankly, it was advantageous to dispose of the whole thing. You just don't do things like that with trademarks. I mean you don't sell part of a trademark and keep a royalty. What we were selling was primarily the trademark, and that's the most valuable part of the whole thing. If you retain an interest in it—a royalty—then you have to pay income tax on it as regular income. It's an involved thing. Also it wouldn't have made very much sense. I have no successor to take it over. I might as well enjoy it now."

Brunot said that, unlike Butts the inventor, he had no emotional feelings or regrets about no longer being involved with Scrabble. "I feel I made the right decision. I would have felt sorry, I'll admit, if Selchow & Righter had done something to the game that wrecked it."

There's another reason why Jim Brunot sold Scrabble, although he doesn't talk about it much. In 1971, about the same time he relinquished all rights to the game, Brunot's wife, Helen, was ill, and she died in 1972. They had played Criss-crosswords together in the late 1930s and early 1940s and had launched Scrabble together in 1948; and, according to Brunot's friends, he idolized his wife. Helen Brunot was the person mainly responsible for rewriting and clarifying Alfred Butts's rules, and it was

Mrs. Brunot who came up with the idea of adding the tiles still in your hand to the total of the player who goes out.

"My wife and I played Scrabble a lot—right up until her death," Jim Brunot said. After she died, you get the impression that Scrabble was no longer such a game to the man who used to always say to business associates, "Gentlemen, it's only a game."

3 A NIGHT ON THE TILES

Some future archaeologist's concept of what life was like in the twentieth century is going to be completely distorted if he unearths a small, flat, smooth, wooden tile with a letter and a number imprinted on one side. The first archaeologist who finds a long-buried Scrabble tile among the relics of past civilizations will be as mystified about former earthlings' printing processes as the twenty-fifth-century earth-prober who digs up a golden arch from a McDonald's hamburger stand and tries to recreate a twentieth-century house.

Scrabble tiles have been readily lost and rarely found in the Grand Canyon, in the Grenadine Islands in the Caribbean, and halfway up a mountain in Japan. Only King Neptune knows how many have been buried in the sand or washed out to sea around Jones Beach and the Hamptons in New York. Jim Brunot estimates there must be "thousands" lost at Jones Beach.

By conservative estimate there are three billion Scrabble tiles in circulation around the world—almost one for every person on the globe—and that doesn't include replacement tiles or the millions of faulty ones discarded by the manufacturers.

How these unmistakable, aesthetically pleasing tiles came about is a story in itself. It involved an improbable search for a grainless wood, which started in Vermont and ended in a Bavarian forest near Adolf Hitler's hideaway at Berchtesgaden in Germany. Jim Brunot described the "find" as being "one of the most fortunate things to happen to us ever—those beautiful wooden tiles made the game stand out. They gave it class." Over the years experimental tiles were made out of plywood, cardboard, plastic, maple, and even the hard redwood used in the handles of carving knives. However, none, despite a strong rumor, were ever made out of ivory for composer-conductor Leonard Bernstein.

The original tiles made by Butts for his Criss-crosswords game were cut out of plywood and then had sheets of colored cardboard glued to the bottom to hide the telltale grain, so that letters could not be readily identified. On top Butts pasted his blueprint letters and then varnished each tile.

When Jim Brunot took over, he had plywood tiles made in East Orange, New Jersey, and handstamped the letters on—one letter at a time, 98 times to a box—on a handpress he and his wife had installed in the garage of their Connecticut home. The tiles in the original sets were rough, occasionally cracked, quite easily identifiable, and surprisingly expensive.

"I didn't know until then," Brunot said, "how most plywood sheeting you buy has faults hidden in it. I discovered there are often holes in the sheets that don't show when you buy a huge piece of it, but certainly show when you cut it down to 3/4-inch squares."

Brunot and his wife kept up the search for the perfect tile. (Years previously Butts had been offered a sample of a sturdy tile by a cutlery handle manufacturer in New Hampshire. The tiles were a burgundy color stamped with gold letters that coincidentally looked surprisingly similar to ones chosen 20 years later by Scrabble tournament organizers.) The Brunots went to Maine and Vermont on a vacation and stopped at woodworking factories along the way in quest of the elusive "tile with class."

"We finally found one place, in Vermont I think it was," Brunot said, "that one place that could make our tiles, or so we thought. They had a machine that had been designed to make little rectangles of wood that were to be used in toy grocery stores. Apparently, the wooden cubes were wrapped in paper to simulate packages of cornflakes and soap powder and things like that and then used to stock the shelves of the toy grocery stores."

Brunot discovered later the tiles were not satisfactory after all. "The shapes were not even; and the tiles, not constant. The finish was poor, and they were frequently marked with a streak of color. It was obvious to anyone who could memorize letters which ones the best tiles were because of the distinctive patterns on the backs."

Finally, a neighbor, who knew of Brunot's tile troubles, came to the rescue. "My neighbor was on vacation in Germany, and he came across this outfit that was making wooden toys that were beautifully finished. It was a small toy factory, and they called it a 'Czechoslovakian finish.' I wrote for some samples. The man's name was Schowanek, and he told me that it was a secret method of finishing that had been invented by his father. Apparently, during the war years the family had fled from Czechoslovakia to East Germany and finally to West Germany to a place called Bad Reichenhall, where they had this small toy factory."

The price for the specialized tiles was too high, according to Brunot, but he realized the quality was so much better than anything else he had ever seen that it was decided to go ahead with the deal and the distinctive Scrabble tile was born.

"When Scrabble became a craze we were importing tiles by the millions, absolute millions," Brunot said. "The demand got so big we had them shipped in bulk cases. We ran into a Customs problem by having the tiles all completed in Germany, by having them cut and stamped there. Customs said they'd have to consider them complete games; so we ended up having the vowels made and stamped in Germany and the rest made there and stamped here. We also wanted to keep the 'made in U.S.A' tag on the game."

The German tiles had one unexpected side effect that brought Brunot bags of mail: the chemical coating used in the glaze finish was relished by dogs. In fact, canines found the taste about as irresistible as cats regard catnip. "We had letter after letter from people asking for replacements because their dog had eaten some of their tiles."

One plaintive letter he received was from a youngster who had received a Scrabble set and a puppy for Christmas. The dog had gorged on the tiles before a game could be played. Another Scrabble player who had lost the battle with his dog advised Brunot that he should get out of the game business and get into the pet food business by packaging his tiles as "doggy dinners." "I still don't know what was in those tiles," Brunot said, "but it was surely potent as far as dogs were concerned."

Which raises another question: What will some future archaeologist deduce if he finds not only a Scrabble tile, but a half-eaten one at that, hidden under the floor of the Grand Canyon? He may think a hardy race that once lived there survived on primitive alphabet soup.

4 THE SCRAMBLE
AFTER SCRABBLE

For 15 years Scrabble had been unmarketable. It had been ridiculed as "unplayable," "too complicated," "too professional," and "unglamorous." But once the Scrabble craze caught fire in 1952, everybody wanted to get into the act.

As Jim Brunot mildly put it, "There was a rash of other games. We had some great copyright fights in the early fifties."

There were more than a dozen different games that flooded on to the market. All were similar enough to Scrabble to attract would-be Scrabble buyers, and most were just different enough to avoid infringement of copyright. Parker Brothers, the makers of Monopoly®, who had twice rejected versions of Scrabble, tried to buy the game from Jim Brunot, according to Alfred Butts. When thwarted, they brought out their own game called Key Word® which incorporated facets of Scrabble and parts of the veteran Selchow & Righter game Parcheesi®. The board and the letters were color-coordinated, and players were permitted to use only designated areas of the playing surface.

At his country home in upstate New York, Alfred Butts has a veritable Scrabble museum, including copies of all the games that imitated the one to which he had given birth. Among the new word games was Score-a-Word, which was described on the box as being "the fascinating new crossword game craze." It wasn't *the* fascinating crossword game craze, but it was worth a try. Another game called Scramble Card Game®, and a third, called Jaymar Crosswords, had premium letter squares like those in Scrabble. "Some of those imitators tried all sorts of things," Butts said, "and none survived. Some didn't even last a year, I don't think."

One of the reasons the imitators were so keen to get into the market was the chronic shortage of genuine Scrabble sets. Brunot's Production & Marketing Company in Connecticut could not keep up with the demand, and there was a waiting list for thousands of sets.

One game that did do well and, in fact, sold more than a million sets was a game called Skip-a-Cross®. It was manufactured in Chicago by a company called Cadaco-Ellis, and its success didn't perturb Brunot at all—he had licensed it. "We hoped that Skip-a-Cross, which was identical to Scrabble but was a cheaper version, would relieve the pressure because we knew we couldn't meet the production demands for Scrabble. I wanted to maintain the quality of the playing pieces of the original game; so I permitted the sale of Skip-a-Cross through cut-rate chain stores. The tiles were cardboard, and they weren't allowed to use the Scrabble name, and it did somewhat relieve the pressure while we caught up."

□

Brunot found himself defending his copyright on all fronts. In Sweden a game, identical to Scrabble and called Alphabet, was marketed before Brunot's copyright could head it off, and periodically he had trouble with a bootlegger who was mass-producing shoddy Scrabble sets in Hong Kong.

"The copyright of the board was the most useful one. We knew that the rules and any textual material like that could be rewritten so as to avoid any copyright infringement, but the board copyright was the most important," Brunot said. Whenever he became aware of a possible infringement, Brunot had his patent lawyers send off a letter. "Usually, a couple of letters from the attorneys would quiet down anything that looked like a copy. One game published in Chicago was an exact replica of our playing surface except that it had a couple of extra rows that made it sort of circular. We started action on that, but it never went to court, and they stopped production, and the game was withdrawn."

Actually, Brunot was forewarned and partly forearmed for copyright problems. Back in 1947, when he and Twitchell were making their deal with Butts, he expressed concern over how many sets of Criss-crosswords were in existence.

Butts said, "I told Jim that I had made about 50 sets, and he asked me to try to get back all the old uncopyrighted games. He was afraid that my making the sets and selling them had put the game in the public domain, and he thought that perhaps somebody else would see a Criss-crossword board and decide they could make a game of it."

Butts did manage to get back a couple of his old games (which he had sold for $1.50) by offering the owners editions of the new game Scrabble. "It was impossible to track them all down. I mean, I'd had orders by letter from people in Washington and Louisiana and Maine. Even some from the Sisters of St. Francis Convent in Rochester, New York. I've still got the letters. I never throw anything away."

Butts's original attempt to copyright his game was quashed because, he said, "they decided I couldn't get a patent on a game that was based on anagrams, which were in the public domain." Then Chester Ives, the Connecticut bookstore owner, had attempted to copyright the Criss-crossword board, but the application had stalled because of a Patent Office dispute over whether or not a blueprint could be copyrighted.

When he took over the game, Brunot, with his own patent attorneys —and no doubt with his Washington connections—went to Washington with Butts and got everything straightened out. "We got Ives's copyright application approved retroactively, and he signed it back over to Butts, and Butts signed it over to us."

Brunot and Twitchell also obtained a letter from Herbert Simonds, the consulting engineer, who had also at one stage almost made a deal with Butts for his original game.

□

Over the years, Brunot, through the Production & Marketing Company, and later Selchow & Righter, maintained and added to their copyrights from 1948 and 1949 through 1953, 1962, and 1974.

More Scrabble-type games were produced by Selchow & Righter, the company that started manufacturing Parcheesi® back in the nineteenth century. Some were deluxe sets of the original Scrabble, but there was also a Scrabble version of anagrams, using cheaper wooden tiles with red lettering. Then came Scrabble Cubes®, incorporating word-building skills with the luck of a dice roll. R.S.V.P.®, another Scrabble brand game, was introduced as a "three-dimensional crossword game." It featured some of the tactics of Scrabble plus the cunning of tic tac toe and was played on an open, upright grid board, with each player filling the latticework with cubed letters. R.S.V.P.® came into it because each player's words read backwards to his opponent, who had to try to turn the inverted letters into a word of his own in reply.

And for players who chafed at the slowness of Scrabble turns, a Scrabble-based game called R.P.M.® was devised. In that one players armed with letter tiles clustered around a board that steadily revolved. Each player, who was also supplied with identifying color chips, tried to complete words before the board spun out of reach.

□

Alfred Mosher Butts never knew what he was starting that Sunday morning over breakfast more than 40 years ago when he said to his wife, "Have a look at this, dear, when you've finished your breakfast . . . I think I've invented a new game."

5 $CRABBLE—THE WORLDWIDE MONEYMAKER

One day in mid-1949, Alfred Butts received his first six-monthly Scrabble royalty check from the game's new owner Jim Brunot. It was for $36.48. Over the next 25 years the checks became bigger and more frequent until, by Brunot's calculation, he had paid Scrabble's inventor more than one million dollars in royalties. Brunot, who lost money in those early sluggish days, admitted that over the years he personally had made "in excess of two million dollars" profit from the game. And Selchow & Righter, the next owners, made and are still making millions more than Butts and Brunot combined.

The game of Scrabble was internationalized more quickly than any American game in history, and consequently it also made fortunes for other manufacturers and distributors who bought the rights to the new craze from Jim Brunot in the early 1950s—men like England's Richard Spear and Australia's Tibor "Tee-are" Urban. In fact, on a population ratio, Scrabble was more popular in Australia and England than it was or is in its land of origin. In Australia, for example, where the total population is only 13 million, Urban's company has sold more than two million sets. The game that sold 59,000 sets down under at $2.95 (Aust.) a set in 1954 is now selling more than double that (124,000 sets in 1974) at $10.00 (Aust.) a game. That's more than $13.50 (U.S.). Urban's success story with Scrabble sounds a bit like Brunot's slow-starting, then accelerated climb up the money ladder. At one stage, according to Urban, he had laid out between £4,000 and £5,000 (more than $7,000) before he had sold "a single, solitary set. My friends thought I was crazy," he said. "They also said I would go quickly broke."

☐

Urban's interest in the game was piqued when a friend returned from a visit to the United States in 1953 and brought home a set of Scrabble. "We played two hands," Urban recalled, "and I quickly found out that the game went against every rule. But I liked it." He liked it so much that he

26

went to a big department store in Sydney called David Jones (the city's equivalent of Macy's), but they had never heard of Scrabble.

Urban wrote to a friend in Chicago who bought a set from Marshall Field's and sent it to Australia. In an accompanying letter, the friend told Urban what a craze Scrabble was in the United States and how difficult it was to buy sets.

Urban, who was born in Hungary and is now in his seventies, migrated to Australia in 1939. He decided he wanted to get into the Scrabble business. Until that time he had run, with a partner, a small production and distributing company that sold torches, cigarette lighters, and cigarette cases. He had never been in the game business. He made contact with Brunot, via Selchow & Righter, and quickly discovered that he wasn't the only person interested in selling Scrabble to Australians.

"I found out that they had 26 applications from Australia, including Frank Packer," Urban said. (Packer, later Sir Frank Packer, was a multimillionaire Australian newspaper magnate, renowned for his tenacity when he wanted something, a trait well illustrated by his repeated, unsuccessful attempts to win the America's Cup at Newport, Rhode Island.)

"I knew everybody would write to Brunot and tell him how big they were . . . how wonderful they were," Urban later told me. "So I wrote and said how small I was. I just put the truth. I said, 'We are a small organization, but if we take up something, we do our best, and in most cases we are quite successful!'"

Urban got the rights—although he almost lost them through nervousness. "I had waited and waited after I wrote, and I had received no reply. I started drafting a second letter. It was pretty strong stuff, demanding to know what was going on. I wanted them to tell me 'Yes or no.' Just as I was showing a draft of the letter to my partner, I got a phone call. We had won."

□

It was then, as he was gearing up for production, that Urban's friends thought he had taken leave of his senses. "Nearly £5,000 I had spent. It was, for that time, a colossal amount of money. It was the equivalent of millions today." The Australian producer of Scrabble had decided early it would be impossible to ship sets in from the United States and too far to bring tiles from Germany. Urban went to a sporting goods manufacturer and asked him if he could copy the tiles. "He looked at the polished German tile I had, and he held up a bead made of similar polished wood," Urban remembered. "He said to me, 'This tile is made by the same people who make these beads. If you can bring me the secret of how they get this finish, I'll take you down to the first notary public you can find, and I will sign over half my factory to you.'" The new Scrabble maker could not come up with the tile formula and instead settled for locally made tiles. Later he switched to plastic.

□

For nearly 20 years Urban paid a percentage of his profits to Brunot—and through him to Butts—and then in 1971 Jim Brunot decided to sell all world rights at the same time as he sold American rights to Selchow & Righter. Tee-are Urban had no hesitation in making a lump payment to Brunot so he could become Mr. Scrabble of Australia.

□

Early in the business, Urban owned Scrabble rights for New Zealand, too, but he found them to be a nuisance and decided to concentrate solely on Australia. He relinquished the New Zealand rights, and they were picked up by Richard Spear, who was accumulating rights for the remainder of the British Commonwealth.

Brunot recalled that he had sold rights in South Africa, "but the first man went broke. Another man took over and did quite well, but eventually Spear took over there too."

Selchow & Righter, the world's biggest producer of Scrabble, does not reveal exact sales figures. Mr. C. E. Tobias, president of the company, said in a letter "... Selchow & Righter is a privately held firm and frankly we prefer to remain as such." However, The New York Times reported in 1973 that Scrabble games constituted "30 to 40 percent of the company's business." And it is known that the company is marketing at least one million sets a year. Lee Tiffany, who works for Selchow & Righter and who is president of the Scrabble® Crossword Game Players®, Inc., said that "30 to 50 million" sets had been sold in the United States alone, "and that does not take in other games like R.S.V.P.,® and Scrabble Cubes,® etc."

The Times article also reported that over the years before it bought Scrabble outright from Brunot, Selchow & Righter paid him "about five percent of the wholesale price" per set. Understandably, Butts and Brunot do not shout their financial positions from the rooftops, although both certainly would be multimillionaires if they had a dollar for every time somebody has said, "You must have made a fortune from that game." People are fascinated by money.

When I asked him the same question, Butts countered, "I'll tell you what I've told other people when they've got inquisitive about the money. I actually got very little royalty on each set. It averaged out to be about three cents a set. Now that sounds like nothing at all, but they're selling a million sets a year. People can't work that out very quickly in their heads. If people think I'm making too much money, they can say 'Well, a million sets a year. I guess he didn't do that for many years.' And the people that think I *ought* to get a lot of money say 'Well, three cents a set for a million sets over several years, well, that's quite a lot of money.' "

Butts added, "I made enough money to buy back my great-great-grandfather's farm and get it back in shape and to buy my apartment in Jackson Heights. Let's say I made enough money that I don't have to worry about it."

Jim Brunot said he couldn't tell you exactly how much he had made from Scrabble—even if he wanted to. "I paid Butts more than a million, and I'm worth more than two million. It's hard to work out though because of other business, you know, things like real estate. It all obviously started with Scrabble though. I was worth about $200,000 at the start. No, less that that really . . . perhaps $100,000."

At the beginning of 1976, the financial involvement in Scrabble ended for both Jim Brunot and Alfred Butts. Selchow & Righter made the final payment of the five-year takeover plan to Brunot, and Brunot made the final payment to Butts. If Scrabble sells another 100 million sets in the next 25 years, neither man will receive a penny.

Said Brunot, "It wouldn't have made sense to hold on to it. I have no successor to take over." He said he had no "emotional regrets" and felt he had made the right decision.

Butts, the inventor, doesn't feel quite the same way. "I didn't want it to end like this. I wanted to continue the royalty as long as it went," he said. "Of course, I got quite a bit more out of the settlement each year for the five final years than I would have got from royalties for those years. But 1976 is the end." Butts is not bitter, and he said, "Don't make a big thing out of this or make it sound like I didn't go along with it. I got money out of it. I suppose it's very corny to say, but you know I got more than money out of it. So many people have come to me and said, 'Oh, it's wonderful we have Scrabble. We're so glad you invented it.' "

Part II

THE RULES OF SCRABBLE

6 WHAT IS SCRABBLE—AND HOW TO PLAY IT

Anyone can play Scrabble.

Two seven-year-olds with a vocabulary no larger than *cat, mat, ma,* and *pa* can have as much fun with the game as two English professors trying to out-alphabet each other with words like *fuzil, mirza, zibet,* and *zooid.* In special editions you can even play Scrabble if you speak only Russian or French or German or Italian. An Arabic edition is in the works, and if you are blind you can play in braille.

If you have ever done a crossword puzzle in your life, then Scrabble is sort of familiar territory (after all, it was first known as Criss-crosswords), and you are also prime Scrabble bait if you have ever unjumbled an anagram or juggled with a cryptogram or deciphered one of those scrambled word games in the daily newspaper. When you boil it down, you are also good Scrabble material if you have ever played Happy Family or Snap or Parcheesi or Pin-the-Tail-on-the-Donkey or poker—or if you've ever read a book or owned a dictionary.

Once you start, you are involved in a game whose roots are in antiquity.

□

The game was not born until the 1930s, but Scrabble's inventor, Alfred Butts, concedes that the sport of deciphering anagrams had a big influence on him—and anagrams go back hundreds of years. The name *anagram* is derived from the ancient Greek *anagrammatismos,* which, admittedly, is a word you won't get much of a chance to use in Scrabble. At least it's proof, though, of just how old word games are.

The beauty of Scrabble is that the game incorporates the goals or styles of several different games. In a way it's like a crossword with each player trying to dovetail seemingly disparate letter combinations into complete words. It also has a hint of that popular old tile game called dominoes—because of the basic rule that no Scrabble tile can be played unless it can mate with a tile already on the board. There's more than a touch of poker's "luck of the draw" when you face the uncertainty of drawing fresh tiles from the deck. And anyone who has unsuccessfully scanned the board looking for a place to attach a seven-letter word can immediately draw an analogy with Pin-the-Tail-on-the-Donkey.

□

So what is Scrabble? It's a mind game in which two, three, or four players, using up to seven lettered tiles at a time, try to build words on a grid-pattern board. As props, you have 100 wooden tiles with letters imprinted on them plus a board containing 225 squares for a playing surface.

Later in this book there are tips on how to play seven-letter "bingo" words, how to make strategic blocks and fades, how to psyche your opponent out of high-scoring plays, and how to make judicious use of alleged problem letters. But none of these foreign-sounding things should scare a Scrabble tenderfoot. Forget, at least for the moment, such things as the cutthroat tactics of Tournament Scrabble and the art of challenging, and forget the "satire syndrome" and the "polecat pass." What you need first are the basics, and what follows here is a step-by-step breakdown on Scrabble for beginners.

□

As I said, anybody of any age and any educational background can play the game and enjoy it. It is true that good Scrabble players regularly score game totals in the high hundreds, and it is also true that two accomplished, highly competitive Scrabblers can expect to score 600 to 800 points between them in any game. Individually, a good Scrabble player should always score more than 300 points in a game, although a tight game, manipulated by a player honed in the art of keeping the board "tight," can inhibit the scoring. I have seen thrilling games played by two polished players where the scoring opportunities were so limited that the combined total just cleared 500.

The following is a scoring target so that you know how you are faring in a two-handed game. The scores are combined.

Starting out:	300–400
Average:	500–600
Good:	600–700
Professional:	700–800
Scrabble Whiz:	800– ?

Before you get discouraged by those high numbers, I should point out one basic Scrabble fact: It doesn't matter if you score only 150 points in a Scrabble game as long as your opponent scores only 149. That's all the game is about. You take the letters from the bag and place them across the grid board in such a way that they score more points than your opponent gets from his letter placement.

For reference purposes and for later recreation of good Scrabble moves, imagine your board is laid out something like a chess board with each square carrying a letter and a number for identification. In Scrabble, the 15 horizontal squares are labeled from *A* through the letter *O* (Board No. 1) with the letters running from left to right. The vertical squares are labeled from No. 1 through No. 15 from top to bottom. The key to this code, and an easy one to remember, is that if a word used is placed horizontally on the board, then the NUMBER is listed first. If the word is vertical, then the code LETTER is listed first.

Take, for example, the word *march* on Board No. 2. It is listed as 8 *F–J* because it starts on the eighth line and runs horizontally from the *F* square through the *J* square. The number is listed first to signal that the word is a horizontal one. If, instead, the word *march* were placed vertically on the board (Board No. 3) with the middle letter *R* still on the center star, then it would be listed as *H* 6–10. The letter is listed first to signify a vertical word and then the numbers 6–10 are given to show that the word runs through those coordinates.

The two things to remember are these: the letters run ACROSS the board from *A* through *O*, and the numbers run DOWN the board from 1 through 15. If a word is placed VERTICALLY, the constant letter is called first, followed by the numbers; and if it is placed HORIZONTALLY, the constant number is called first followed by the letters. This form of keeping track of each move is used in Tournament Scrabble.

Although the idea for such a board configuration obviously comes from chess, I'll admit I first thought of it by remembering a childhood game called Crush the Nazi Navy. It was a pencil-and-paper game—still played in the United States under the name Battleship—in which the letters *c–r–u–s–h a–d–o–l–f* were written down one side of a sheet of paper and the numbers 1–10 were filled in along the bottom. Each player had one of those gridded paper oceans, and on it he hid his "navy" by drawing lines of various lengths, signifying battleships. To score hits on your opponent's ships, you called out letter and number combinations, which he had to mark with a cross on his sheet. Any time the coordinates touched a hidden ship, you scored a "hit."

The hits you score in Scrabble are influenced by the number of letters you use in the words you make, the values of the letters you use to make

BOARD NO. 1

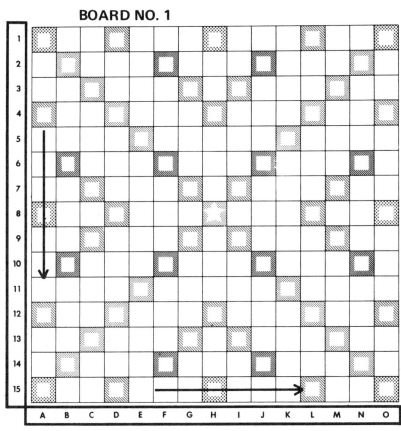

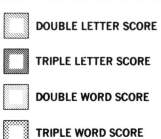

DOUBLE LETTER SCORE

TRIPLE LETTER SCORE

DOUBLE WORD SCORE

TRIPLE WORD SCORE

BOARD NO. 2

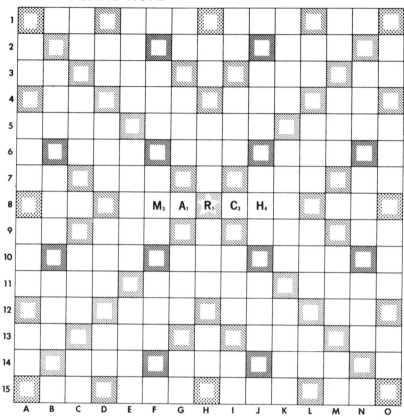

DOUBLE LETTER SCORE

TRIPLE LETTER SCORE

DOUBLE WORD SCORE

TRIPLE WORD SCORE

BOARD NO. 3

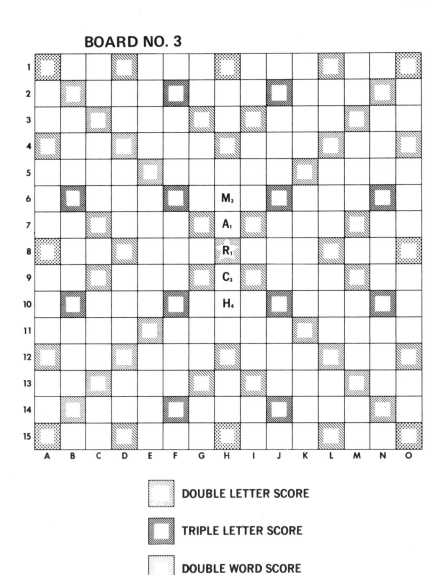

DOUBLE LETTER SCORE

TRIPLE LETTER SCORE

DOUBLE WORD SCORE

TRIPLE WORD SCORE

them, and your placement of the tiles on the board, using the premium squares to collect extra points. The letter values range from a single point for an *E*, of which there are 12 in the set, to a high point of 10 each for the solitary *Z* and the single *Q*. There are also two blank tiles to be used as "wild cards." By themselves they have a face value of zero, but, as you will discover later, they are two of the most valuable tiles in the game. On the diagrammed boards, blank tiles are always represented by heavy outline. The following is a list of all the letters in the alphabet plus their frequency in the Scrabble set and each letter's face value:

LETTER	NUMBER IN SET	VALUE
A	9	1
B	2	3
C	2	3
D	4	2
E	12	1
F	2	4
G	3	2
H	2	4
I	9	1
J	1	8
K	1	5
L	4	1
M	2	3
N	6	1
O	8	1
P	2	3
Q	1	10
R	6	1
S	4	1
T	6	1
U	4	1
V	2	4
W	2	4
X	1	8
Y	2	4
Z	1	10
blank	2	0

It will help your game if you know something about how the letter distribution came about and why inventor Butts arbitrarily decided there should be 12 tiles imprinted with the letter *E* and only four, say, with the letter *S*. Butts takes a lot of pride in the fact that when Jim Brunot started to market his game 15 years after its invention, he kept the same letter distribution and the same letter values that were designated by Butts when he was hand-pasting paper letters onto plywood squares in the thirties. "Back then I thought that listing the letter distribution on the board was important, too, so that people could keep track of what had been played," Butts said, "and obviously Jim Brunot thought so, too."

Several things influenced Butts in the way he portioned out the 100 tiles and the values he gave each letter. "I had played a lot of anagrams, and I was keen on crosswords, and around that time there was also the fad of cryptograms, and I was interested in them too. I knew that the letter *E* was the most commonly used letter in the alphabet; so it had to be in there more than others. I also went for a lot of *I* tiles because of the opportunities for good endings with *ing* and *ion*. I had trouble with the letter S because I wanted to have a fair number of them, but I didn't want to make it too easy for people just to pluralize every word by adding an S to words on the board. I decided on four, which is abnormally low, but the two blanks sort of compensated for that because they can be used as esses too."

Butts also penalized the S by giving it a low face value.

□

Apart from the face value points that you automatically pick up when you play a tile, you can also reap huge benefits by exploiting the "premium squares" permanently affixed to the board, as shown on Board No. 4. There are squares which, if you land on them, triple your score for the entire word or words you have just played. Other premium squares can double the value of the word or double or even triple a single letter in the last-played word. The importance of these premium squares is obvious: without them the value of the entire 100 tiles would only add up to 185.

People score in the hundreds (up to 300 in a single turn) by strategically placing their tiles on the triple-word score squares (there are eight of them), on the double-word score squares (there are 16 of them), or on the pink center square marked by a star, which, besides being the starting point for the game, also means a double-word tally for the lucky starter. Scores are also boosted by landing on a triple-letter square, which means you multiply by three the face value of the specific letter that covers the square. There are 12 triple-letter squares and 24 double-letter squares, for which you multiply by two the face value of the landing tile.

If, in a single turn, you land on a double-letter square with one letter

BOARD NO. 4

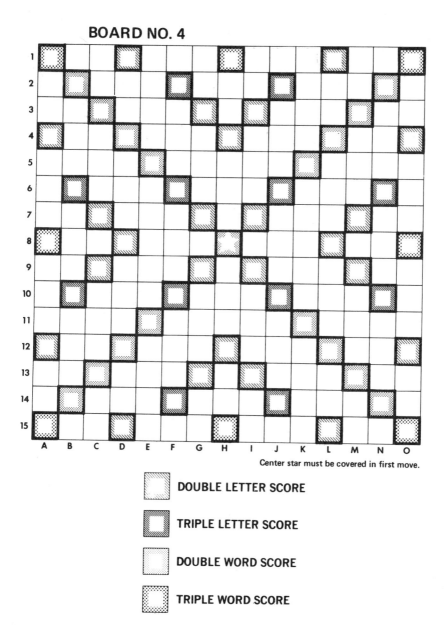

Center star must be covered in first move.

DOUBLE LETTER SCORE

TRIPLE LETTER SCORE

DOUBLE WORD SCORE

TRIPLE WORD SCORE

and another lands on a double-word square, the double-letter square is counted first and then the double-word tally is made. This sequence is important.

The triple-word squares, which are painted in each corner of the board and on the edges of an imaginary four-pointed cross, are easy to spot—they are painted bright red. The double-word squares are pink (like the center star), the triple-letter squares are dark blue, and the double-letter squares are pale blue.

□

To reach these high-scoring squares, each player, in turn, can lay down any number of the seven tiles that he has in his rack. He can drop all seven letters as long as they make a word and as long as any letters or words that they touch and that are already on the board still constitute complete words. Or the player can place only a single letter on the board to change somebody else's previously played word into a different word. (After each turn, the player draws as many tiles as he has just played to replenish his rack and to keep his tile supply at seven at all times.)

The only restrictions when placing tiles on the board are these: (1) The player can only place tiles in one direction in any one turn. He can place tiles horizontally (Board No. 5) or vertically (Board No. 6) to make words. He cannot place tiles diagonally (Board No. 7). (2) At least one letter of the newly played word must attach to at least one letter already on the board; and after the play, all letter combinations, including the new word, the old word, and any other letters involved, must spell out legitimate words.

The game looks like a crossword puzzle as the interlocking words are formed. Only in this version the clues are all in your head and in your rack. What words you form are completely up to you except for such things as proper nouns, abbreviations, most foreign words, and words with hyphens and apostrophes. These categories of banned words are spelled out in the standard Scrabble rules in the lid of your Scrabble set and are discussed in the next chapter.

To start the game, each player draws one tile. The original Scrabble rules direct players to place all 100 tiles face down on the table before the game and to draw from there whenever tiles are required. A popular alternative, played in Tournament Scrabble and at my Scrabble table, is to use a cloth bag to hold the tiles. After each player has drawn a single letter, he turns it face up, and the one who has drawn the tile nearest the start of the alphabet gets to start the game. If in a two-man game both players draw the same letter, then they must redraw. If more than two players are involved, then only the ones who have tied in the draw get to pick again,

BOARD NO. 5

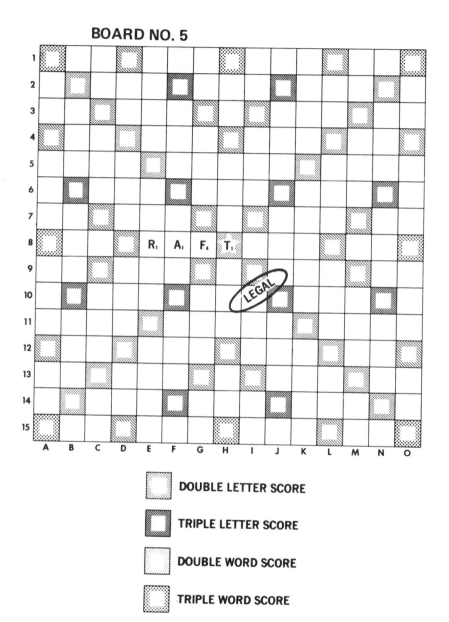

DOUBLE LETTER SCORE

TRIPLE LETTER SCORE

DOUBLE WORD SCORE

TRIPLE WORD SCORE

BOARD NO. 6

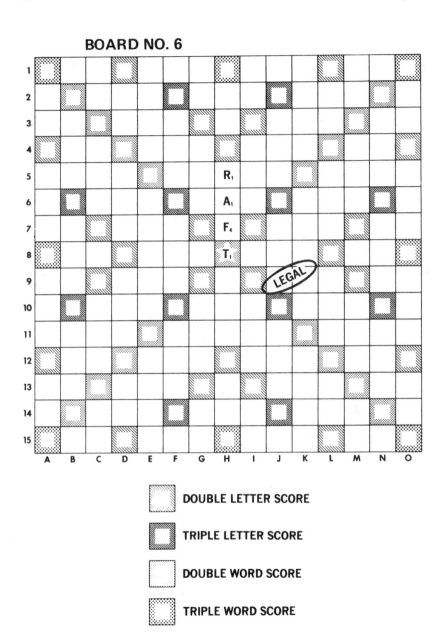

DOUBLE LETTER SCORE

TRIPLE LETTER SCORE

DOUBLE WORD SCORE

TRIPLE WORD SCORE

BOARD NO. 7

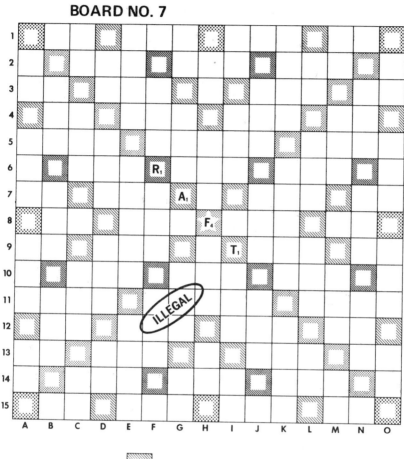

DOUBLE LETTER SCORE

TRIPLE LETTER SCORE

DOUBLE WORD SCORE

TRIPLE WORD SCORE

and the final jockeying to see who starts first is only between those players. If a player draws the blank, then that is considered the best letter in the alphabet, and he starts. These tiles drawn to determine the "pole position" are then put back in the pool—on the table or in the bag—and reshuffled. All players then draw seven fresh tiles, sight unseen.

There are different rules for starts (see the chapter on game variations), but the standard beginning is for the starter to place any word on the board as long as it consists of two or more letters and as long as one of those letters covers the star in the middle of the board.

In the sample game on Board No. 8, the first player places the word *raft* on the board, making sure that one letter covers the center star. He could play the word horizontally, but, quite legally, runs it down the middle of the board.

For that move the player gets the total of all the face values of his four played tiles, which add up to 7 points. None of his tiles land on premium word squares, but because he has started and because one tile, in this case the letter *T*, covers the center star, his word score is automatically doubled, and he scores a total of 14 points for the move.

His score is recorded on a scorepad, but before this is done, the opposing player (or players if you are playing a three- or four-man game) has the right to challenge that fact that *raft* is indeed a word. If the challenged word does not appear in whatever dictionary is being used as the "house Bible," then the player must pick up his tiles, his score is disallowed, and he forfeits his turn. In basic Scrabble there is no penalty for the challenger if somebody challenges a word and the word is found to be legitimate, and in some of the older sets in which rules have not been updated there is no regulation for the challenged person to miss his turn after removing the erroneous word from the board. However, in tournament play and most accepted house rules, the challenger who loses a dispute must then forfeit his own next turn. This makes challenging an important part of Scrabble strategy, and how, when, and why you challenge are detailed in the strategy section of this book.

Once a word is down and the score has been tallied and recorded, it cannot be moved from that position or removed from the board, even if for some reason, it is later discovered that the word does not really exist.

The first player then draws four fresh tiles, again sight unseen, from the tile bag to bring his rack back up to the standard seven tiles. The second player then gets to move. He has the following options: If he has the necessary tiles, he can extend the word *raft* at either end or at both ends to create words like *craft*, *crafty*, *rafts*, or *rafter*. Or using tiles in his rack and letters already on the board, he can build a totally new word as long as one of his letters hooks on to some part of the existing word.

BOARD NO. 8

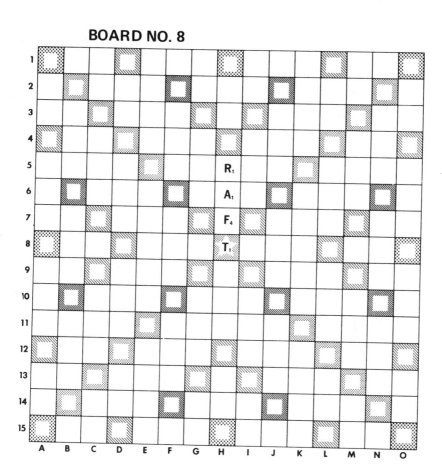

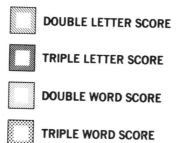

DOUBLE LETTER SCORE

TRIPLE LETTER SCORE

DOUBLE WORD SCORE

TRIPLE WORD SCORE

Player No. 2 plays the horizontal word *strand* on Board No. 9, using the letters S, R, A, N, and D from his own hand and utilizing the T placed on the board previously by his opponent. For that he scores 9 points. He gets 4 points for the letter D because it lands on a double-letter square and the D has a face value of 2 points, and he gets 1 point each for the s–t–r–a–n. You will notice that he still gets the credit for the face value of the T even though the letter was put there by his opponent. If, however, the T had been originally placed on a double-word square or a double-letter square, those premiums would not have been assessed again.

Once a premium square has been covered, and this applies to double- and triple-word squares as well, it is moot. Only the face values of tiles are counted in any later action.

Whether or not Player No. 2 should have played that word at all is a different story, and that is discussed in detail in the strategy part of the book. What we are interested in here is getting a game going.

For example, though, if, instead of playing the word *strand*, the player had added the word *sand* in Board No. 10 to the top of the existing word, he would have scored far better. He would have turned the word *raft* into the word *draft* and would have counted the D as a double-letter score going each way. He would have also received full marks, at face value, of the r–a–f–t vertically plus the double-letter tally for the D as well as the total for the word *sand* horizontally. This is a major scoring point in Scrabble. Anytime you alter an existing word on the board, you receive credit for the new word's complete face value—no matter how much of it was placed there previously by an opponent.

Playing the word *sand* and turning *raft* into *draft* would have given Player No. 2 a score of 18. You will notice the player would have received 4 points for the D in his word *sand* (2 × 2) and then would have received another 4 points for the D in the vertical word *draft* because both ways the letter hit a double-letter square. Indicatively, his score would have been 11 points for amending the existing word and 7 for his new word. So you can see that exploiting an opponent's word is a basic Scrabble tactic. The reason Player No. 2 did not receive any points from the original word *raft* was that his ultimate word *strand* did not change the original word at all even though it was attached to both sides of it.

Anyway let's ignore what the second player could have done and concentrate on what he did do. The board now has *raft* going vertically and the word *strand* intersecting it.

The first player, with his rack restocked, now does what is called tightening the board. By using just a few letters, he weaves his new word through letters already on the board and scores points in all directions. In Board No. 11 he plays the word *most* vertically so that it involves both of

BOARD NO. 9

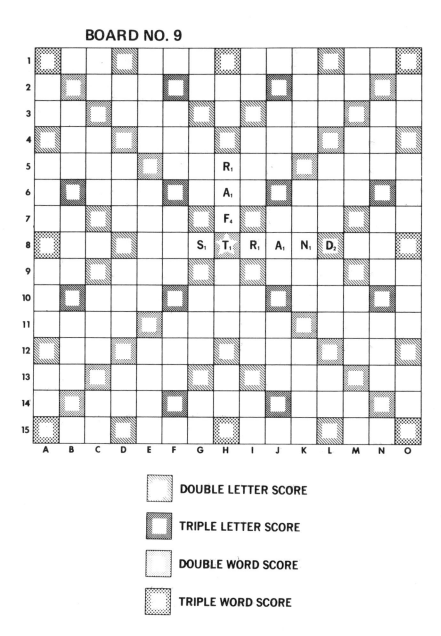

DOUBLE LETTER SCORE

TRIPLE LETTER SCORE

DOUBLE WORD SCORE

TRIPLE WORD SCORE

BOARD NO. 10

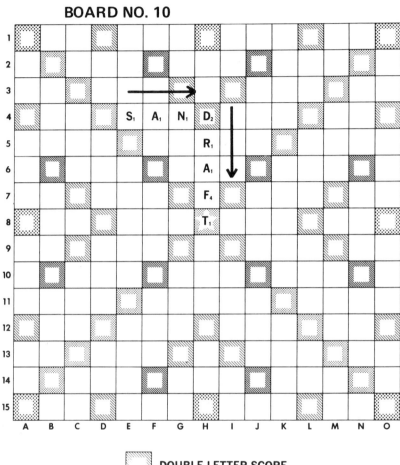

| | S₁ | A₁ | N₁ | D₂ |
| R₁ |
| A₁ |
| F₄ |
| T₁ |

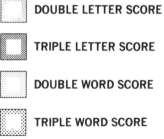

DOUBLE LETTER SCORE

TRIPLE LETTER SCORE

DOUBLE WORD SCORE

TRIPLE WORD SCORE

BOARD NO. 11

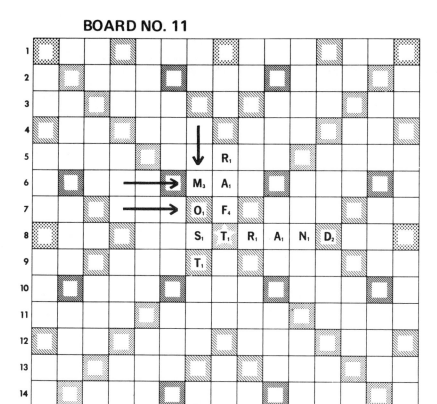

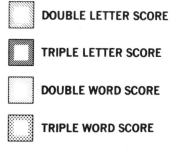

DOUBLE LETTER SCORE

TRIPLE LETTER SCORE

DOUBLE WORD SCORE

TRIPLE WORD SCORE

the existing words on the board and creates three new ones. He gets 7 points from the word *most*, including 3 for the *M*, 2 for the *O* because it hits a double-letter square, 1 for the *S* already on the board, and 2 for the *T* because it also covers a double-letter square. But by placing those tiles snugly against the existing ones, Player No. 1 has also created the word *ma* horizontally and the word *of* horizontally; so he must get credit for those words, too. He gets 4 points for *ma* (which means his three-point *M* has actually been worth 6 points), and he gets 6 points for the word *of*.

His total for the turn is *most*, 8 points; *ma*, 4; *of*, 6; total, 18 points. This is added to his first turn score of 14 to give him a cumulative score of 32.

Player No. 2, now trailing, has luckily drawn the *Z*, one of the four big guns, while restocking his hand. The other three most valued letters are the *Q*, *X*, and *J*. Although he missed the word *draft*, he pounces on the same opportunity this turn in Board No. 12 and turns *raft* into *craft* while making the word *crazy* across the top. He doesn't have a letter *Y* in his hand, but he does have one of the two blanks so he calls that a *Y*.

When a blank lands on a double-letter score, it is meaningless. A blank is worth zero, and zero doubled is still zero. However, when a blank lands on a double-word square or a triple-word square, it most definitely counts—as it does in this case. This move is a good one, and gets Player No. 2 a total of 49 points.

The breakdown is like this. For the word *crazy*, he gets 6 points for the *C* (it lands on a double-letter square), 1 point each for the *R* and the *A*, 10 points for the *Z*, and nothing for the blank substituting for the letter *Y*. That is a total of 18, which is doubled because the blank is on a pink double-word square. He also gets another 6 points for the *C* going vertically in the word *craft* plus 7 points for the face value of *raft*. A total of 49.

Unless you are playing a variation of the game called Ecology Scrabble, in which the blank can be used again and again, then the substitute *Y* remains there for the rest of the game and for the remainder must remain as a *Y*.

Player No. 2 now adds his 49 points to his opening 9 to take the lead with 58 for two turns. Player No. 1, possibly caught with bad letters and an abundance of such low-scoring tiles as two or three *O*'s, tries to get rid of them. He can, at any time, use a turn to "pass" and return any or all of his letters into the bag for a fresh draw. This is explained in detail—the how, when, and why of it—in the strategy section. If a player wishes to redraw, he forfeits his turn, places the no longer wanted tiles face down next to his rack, and draws a corresponding number of fresh tiles from the bag. The unwanted tiles are then placed back in the bag, and the other player gets

BOARD NO. 12

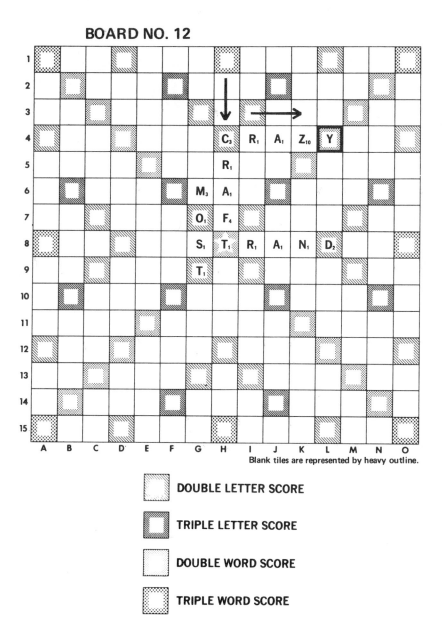

Blank tiles are represented by heavy outline.

DOUBLE LETTER SCORE

TRIPLE LETTER SCORE

DOUBLE WORD SCORE

TRIPLE WORD SCORE

to go again. Instead of passing, though, Player No. 1 decides to "dump" some of his offending tiles—he accepts a low score to get rid of tiles of which he has more than one of a kind in his hand. On Board No. 13 he plays the word *tool*, tucking it up under the previously played *strand*.

For that he gets 5 points for *tool* (the *L* is doubled because it hits a double-letter square), and he gets points for making the short vertical words *at*, *no*, and *do*. He gets 2 points for *at*, 2 for *no*, and although the *D* of his third word *do* is on a double-letter square, it is only scored at face value because it was played in a previous turn and the double count was used then. The total score for his four words is only 12, but he gets to draw four fresh tiles.

His opponent has the letters, *E, E, C, I, L, N, S* in his hand. On Board No. 14 he unjumbles them to make the word *license* and rearranges them again to get the word *silence*. He finally returns to *license*, running the word down the board and pluralizing *tool*. For that he gets 17 points for the word *license* (the *C* and final *E* hit triple-letter squares), and he gets 5 points for the word *tools*. He also gets a bonus of 50 points because he used all seven letters in his hand for what is called a "bingo." So his total score for the turn is 17 for *license*, 50 for the "bingo," and 5 for *tools* for a total of 72. If he had played the word *silence* (Board No. 15), he would have got slightly more because it would have run down into a double-word score for a total of 22 plus 50 for the "bingo" plus 5 points for *tools* for a total of 77. However, that would have left an enticing opening for a good triple-word score for his opponent, as indicated by the arrow on Board No. 15. With the *E* in such a position, he would also have opened the risk of his opponent playing out all seven of his letters to hit *two* triple-word scores. When that happens, a score is tripled and retripled, which means the original total is multiplied by nine. That is the one move that can produce a score of more than 200 and sometimes as high as or even higher than 300 in a single turn. Careful defensive positioning of letters—as described here—will be discussed in greater detail in the strategy section.

And so the game goes with each player filling in the crossword, building off his own previous turns and his opponent's, and replenishing his rack from the bag until the supply of tiles is depleted.

The game can end in either of two ways: (1) With no tiles left in the bag, one player uses up all the remaining tiles in his rack and goes out, play immediately stops, or (2) Both players still have tiles in their racks but cannot find any place on the board where the remaining letters can be placed to make words. This often happens when players are caught with tricky consonants near the end and especially if one is caught with the *Q* and has no *U* to go with it.

If the first ending occurs, the players with tiles remaining have the

BOARD NO. 13

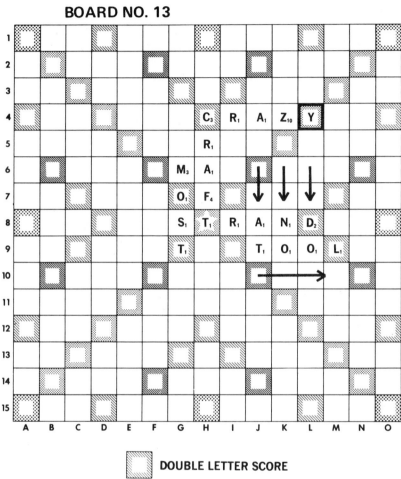

■ DOUBLE LETTER SCORE

■ TRIPLE LETTER SCORE

■ DOUBLE WORD SCORE

■ TRIPLE WORD SCORE

BOARD NO. 14

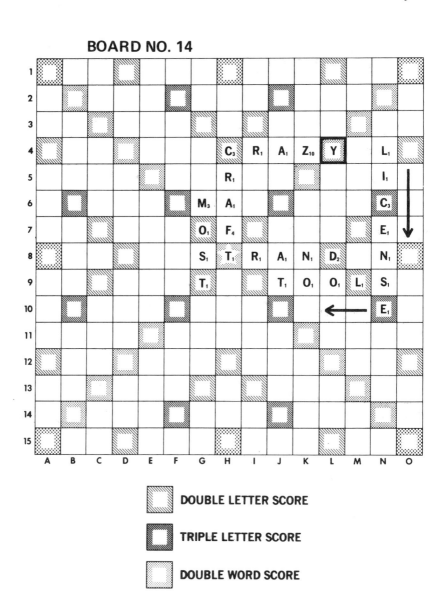

DOUBLE LETTER SCORE

TRIPLE LETTER SCORE

DOUBLE WORD SCORE

TRIPLE WORD SCORE

BOARD NO. 15

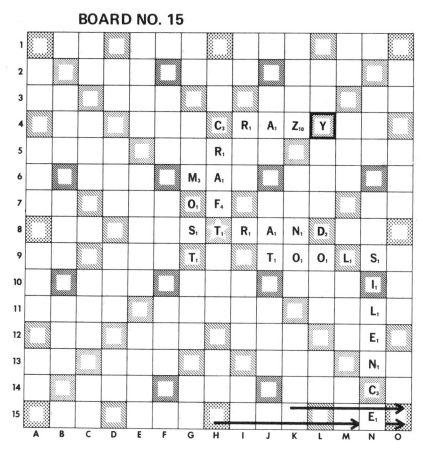

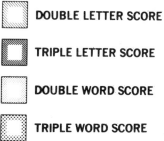

DOUBLE LETTER SCORE

TRIPLE LETTER SCORE

DOUBLE WORD SCORE

TRIPLE WORD SCORE

face values of these tiles deducted from their total scores. The player who went out has his score increased by the value of opponents' tiles still unplayed. A common variation of this is for the player who goes out to receive double the face value of the opponent's remaining tiles while the other player deducts nothing from his own hand. Once a player goes out, all play stops even if an opponent has an opening for his remaining tiles. Some people do play under a house rule that going out first is unimportant and the game continues until anybody and everybody who can make a move has gone.

If the second ending occurs and no player can shed all his tiles, then each player deducts his own remaining tiles from his total.

The person with the highest total at the end, after all the accounting has been done, is the winner, even if another player was the one who physically went out first.

7   BASIC SCRABBLE RULES

Scrabble is a crossword style game best played by two people but is also entertaining with three or a maximum of four players. One person can play Solitaire Scrabble, and this and other versions mentioned in the following rules are detailed in the chapter on variations.

The object of the game is to form interlocking words, crossword fashion, on a special gridded Scrabble board, using lettered tiles. There are 100 tiles in the set, and all of them, except two blank tiles, have specific values printed on them in the botton right-hand corner of each tile.

Players take turns at constructing words on the board from tiles in their racks. Who gets the highest cumulative score is determined by the skill of each player in getting maximum benefit from high-value tiles and from placing them on special bonus squares known as premium squares.

The combined total score for a game should range between 500 and 800 points.

To Start

All 100 tiles should be turned face down on the table and thoroughly shuffled. Unplayed tiles remain face down on the table as a "tile pool" throughout the game. As mentioned earlier, a popular alternative is to place all the tiles in a deep, cloth bag and to use that as a receptacle. It is imperative, whichever method is used, to make sure the tile faces remain hidden until drawn from the pool and played on the board.

Each player draws one tile to determine who gets the privilege of starting the game. The player drawing the letter nearest the beginning of the alphabet starts the game. If two players draw the same low letter, they get to redraw. If a player draws the blank, it is considered the best tile, and he starts even if another player draws an A.

The "starting position" tiles are then all returned to the tile bag or tile heap and reshuffled. One variation of this is for each player to have the choice of rejecting the first tile or keeping it. Starting with the lead-off player and rotating to the left, each player now draws seven new tiles (or six if you are playing the start variation), and the tiles are placed on the racks in front of each player.

The Play

1. The Opening. Using two or more of his letters, the first player forms a word and places it on the board either horizontally or vertically. Horizontal words must read from left to right, and vertical words must read from top to bottom. Diagonal words are not permitted. The only restriction on the starting player's positioning for his word is that one letter, any letter, must cover the center star square. Some house rules set minimums for the length of the starting word, ranging from four letters up to seven letters, and this variation, called "Jacks to Open" or "Aces to Open," is explained in the variations chapter.

As a starting bonus for covering the center star the first player gets to double his total score for the word. If he wishes, however, or if he does not have a word to play, he may forfeit his turn and Player No. 2 gets the chance to start the game. Under that circumstance, the second player would get the starting bonus. The first player who passes may use that turn to exchange any, or all, of the tiles in his rack.

2. Completing a Turn. A player finishes his turn by adding up his score for that move and announcing it before entering it on a tally sheet. He then draws as many new tiles as he has played to bring his rack back up to the original seven tiles. This restocking procedure must be done immediately after each turn and should become automatic.

3. Successive Moves. Play passes to the left. Player No. 2—and then each successive player—adds one or more letters to those already on the board to form a new word or new words, as on Board No. 16. All letters played in any single turn must be placed in one row across or down the board. At least one new letter must touch a letter already on the board. Letters can be placed at either end of existing words or in the middle, if space is available, or as links to join several letter groupings into one word as on Board No. 17. On Board No. 16 a player has used the letter *H* from the word *arch* to make the vertical word *heal*; the letter *L* from *heal* has been utilized in making the horizontal word *lend*, and the *D* from *lend* has been used in constructing the vertical word *good*. Then, on Board No. 17, a player has legally used an *M* at the start of the word *arch* plus the letters *I*, *N* in the middle to tie up with an existing *G* to make the word *marching*.

BOARD NO. 16

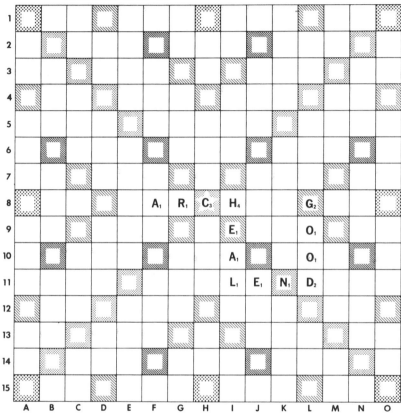

DOUBLE LETTER SCORE

TRIPLE LETTER SCORE

DOUBLE WORD SCORE

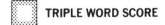
TRIPLE WORD SCORE

BOARD NO. 17

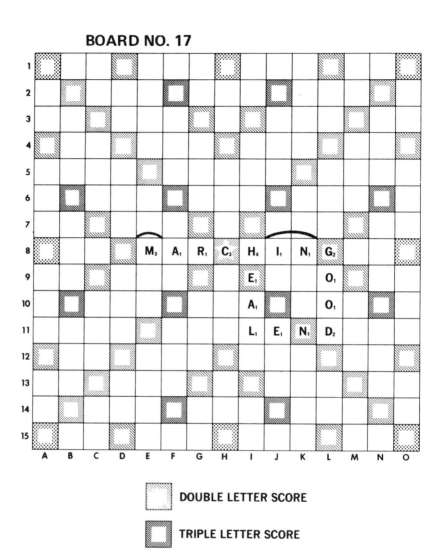

DOUBLE LETTER SCORE

TRIPLE LETTER SCORE

DOUBLE WORD SCORE

TRIPLE WORD SCORE

The same thing applies on Board No. 18, where in two turns *heal* becomes *health* and *lend* becomes *blending*.

Any time letters are placed on the board, they must form a complete word or words; and if, at the same time they touch other letters in adjacent rows, they must also, crossword fashion, form complete words with those letters, no matter if they are horizontal or vertical. As long as that stipulation is honored, players can place parallel words like the example on Board No. 19.

4. Letter Placement. Once a letter has been played, it may not be shifted. The only exception is when you are playing such variations as Anagram Scrabble or Ecology Scrabble, and even then the exception must be spelled out before the start of the game.

5. Blank Tiles. The two blank tiles are "wild cards," which may be used as any letter. When playing a blank, the player must announce what letter it represents. It cannot be shifted or have its designation changed for the remainder of the game. The exception is when you are playing Ecology Scrabble, in which blanks may be recycled again and again.

6. Passing. Any player may use his turn, as mentioned in Rule No. 1, to replace any or all of the letters in his rack. He does this by discarding the unwanted letters face down alongside his rack. He draws the same number of new letters from the tile bag or tile pool, checks to make sure he has drawn the correct number, then discards the old letters back into the pool and shuffles. He may not touch the board or play a word as part of a passing turn. Passing may be done, in turn, at any time until there are only seven letters or less in the pool. After that point is reached, passing, without an exchange of tiles, is permitted, but all letter-changing is banned. After passing, a player awaits his next scheduled turn.

An unusual passing variation, played under some house rules, permits a player to throw back tiles without penalty after restocking his rack if he has three or more of the same letters in his hand. Under this variation, he may throw back all duplicates, in excess of two, without penalty and draw fresh tiles.

If any player passes for three consecutive turns, he forfeits the game. If all players pass three times consecutively, then the game is terminated. Each player deducts the face values of his seven tiles from his total, and the player with the highest score remaining wins the game.

7. Words. Any words found in a standard dictionary (you should agree on which one before you start) are permitted except the following:

BOARD NO. 18

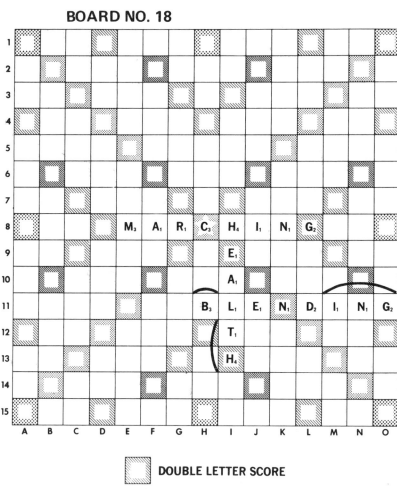

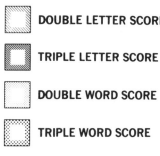

DOUBLE LETTER SCORE

TRIPLE LETTER SCORE

DOUBLE WORD SCORE

TRIPLE WORD SCORE

BOARD NO. 19

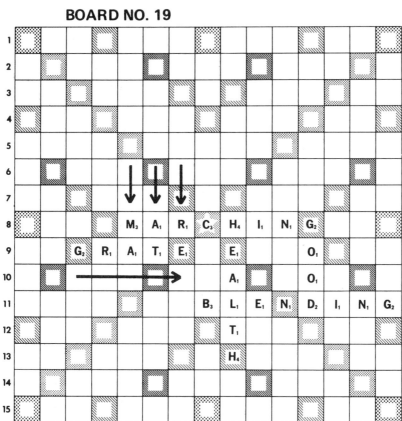

DOUBLE LETTER SCORE

TRIPLE LETTER SCORE

DOUBLE WORD SCORE

TRIPLE WORD SCORE

Proper names
Words that are capitalized, including months and days of the
    week
Words designated as foreign words
Abbreviations
Words requiring apostrophes
Words requiring hyphens.

Words that take normal declensions, comparatives, and superlatives, are permitted even if not in a dictionary if the book of reference spells out the fact, as usually is the case, that you may assume normal transformation unless otherwise stipulated.

8. Challenging. Any word may be challenged once it is on the board and before the next player starts his turn. In a three- or four-handed game, only one of the opponents need challenge. If the word challenged is unacceptable, the player takes back his tiles, forfeits the points he would have scored for that turn, and loses his turn. If the challenge fails, the word stays, the player gets his score, and the game continues. Under standard Scrabble rules there is no penalty for a player who challenges a word and loses the challenge. However, the most prevalent challenge rule—used by a lot of good players and in all tournaments—stipulates that if a challenger fails to uphold his challenge, he forfeits his next turn as a penalty. In a multihanded game all players who joined in the challenge would forfeit their turn. Another, more vicious, variation is for an unsuccessful challenger not only to lose a turn, but also to be penalized by the number of points the disputed play is worth.

The dictionary may not be used for browsing and can only be consulted to settle legal challenges. A word must be challenged before the next player starts his turn. If it escapes detection, a phony word remains on the board and is scored normally. The word can be challenged later if modified by a subsequent play. In that circumstance, however, the modifier takes full responsibility for the original root word. A disputed word cannot be traced back to its source.

9. The End. Play continues until all the tiles have been drawn and one player has used all of his final seven letters. If no player can go out, play stops by mutual agreement after each player has played his rack to a standstill.

Scoring

1. The Scorer. One player is elected scorer and keeps a cumulative tally of each player's score. Ideally, each player should keep a pad and pencil in front of him and keep track of all scores, but most people usually leave the job to the player who is quickest at arithmetic.

2. The Scoring Procedure. The score for each turn is calculated by adding up the face values of all the letters in all the words formed or modified in the play and then adding bonus points scored by landing tiles on "premium squares."

3. Premium Letter Squares. Premium letter bonus squares are shown on Board No. 20. A light blue square *doubles* the score of a letter placed on it; a dark blue square *triples* the score of a letter placed on it.

4. Premium Word Squares. Premium word bonus squares are shown on Board No. 21. The score for the entire *word* is *doubled* when one of its letters lands on a light red square. When a letter lands on a dark red square, the score for the entire *word* is *tripled*. Premiums, if any, for double- or triple-letter squares should be included in the score before the word total is doubled or tripled.

5. Double Bonuses. When two or more words are formed in the same move and when a letter on a premium square features in both the horizontal and vertical words, then the common letter is counted with full bonus value in each direction (see Board No. 22). In this case, the letter *K* is worth 15 points for landing on a triple-letter square in the word *think*, which is then doubled because the letter *T* lands on a double-word square. However, the *K* is also worth 15 points for extending *pin* into *pink* as well as for collecting the face value of the letters *P*, *I*, *N*.

6. Other Bonuses. If a word is formed that covers two premium word squares, the score is doubled and then redoubled (see Board No. 23) for four times the letter count, or it is tripled and then *retripled* nine times the letter count, as the case may be. Although most of the premium word squares are more than seven squares apart, you can reach more than one in a turn by using tiles already on the board as stepping stones.

As mentioned earlier, the center star is a light red square and therefore doubles the total of the opening word score.

BOARD NO. 20

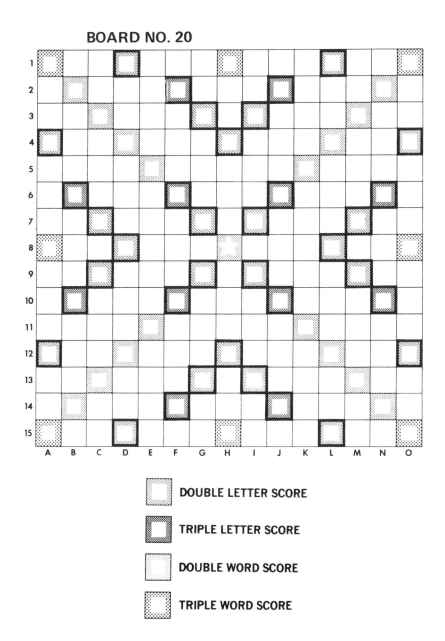

DOUBLE LETTER SCORE

TRIPLE LETTER SCORE

DOUBLE WORD SCORE

TRIPLE WORD SCORE

BOARD NO. 21

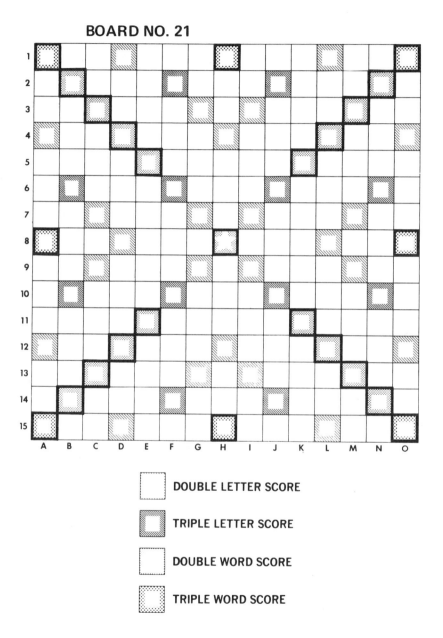

DOUBLE LETTER SCORE

TRIPLE LETTER SCORE

DOUBLE WORD SCORE

TRIPLE WORD SCORE

BOARD NO. 22

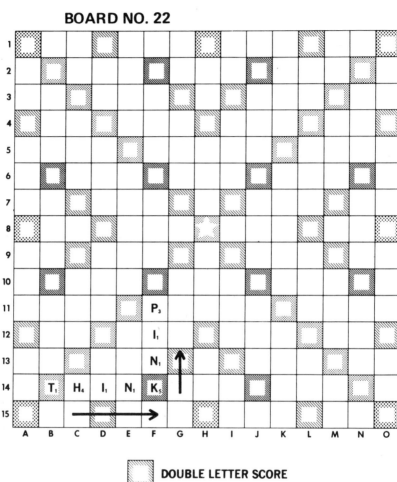

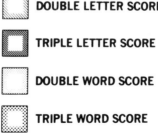

DOUBLE LETTER SCORE

TRIPLE LETTER SCORE

DOUBLE WORD SCORE

TRIPLE WORD SCORE

BOARD NO. 23

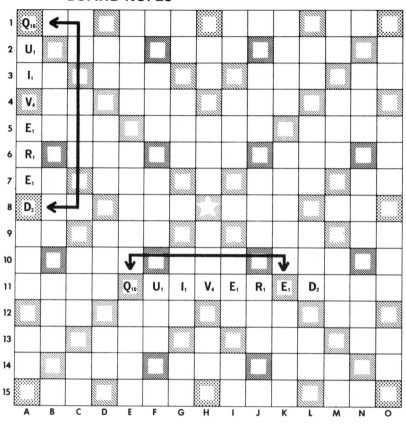

DOUBLE LETTER SCORE

TRIPLE LETTER SCORE

DOUBLE WORD SCORE

TRIPLE WORD SCORE

7. Limits on Premiums. The letter and word premiums apply only in the turn in which they are first played. Once covered, they score at face value only.

8. The Blanks. The blank tiles are basically worth zero points. If a blank tile lands on a double- or triple-letter square, the value is still zero. Twice nothing is nothing. However, if a blank lands on a double-word premium square or a triple-word premium square, the sum of the letters in the word are doubled or trebled even though the blank is valueless by itself.

9. Bingos. Any player who plays out all seven letters in his rack in a single turn scores a bonus of 50 points. The bonus is added after all other tallying for the turn has been completed. If, for example, a player scores a bingo with a tile value of 40 points, which then doubles to 80 because he lands on a double-word square, he then adds the bonus 50 for a total of 130. He does not add the 50-point bonus to the original 40 before doubling for a final score of 180. Any number of bingos can be scored in a game, and a player gets his 50-point bonus each time. The bingo bonus is for dropping all seven tiles at once, and therefore you can get only one bonus per turn—no matter how many words are formed by your seven-letter drop.

10. Final Scoring. At the end of the game each player's score is reduced by the total face values of tiles still in his hand. If one player has used all his letters, then his score is increased by the sum of the unplayed letters in his opponents' racks. A common ending variation is for players not to deduct the residual tiles from their own scores, but for the player who goes out to increase his score by double the face values of the unplayed letters of all the other players.

11. The Winner. The player with the highest score wins the game.

8   TOURNAMENT SCRABBLE

ONE HUNDRED YEARS FROM NOW I WON'T BE HERE
AND YOU WON'T BE HERE . . . BUT SCRABBLE WILL
STILL BE HERE.

—Lee Tiffany, President,
Scrabble® Crossword Game Players®, Inc.

If, as Mr. Tiffany confidently predicts, Scrabble *is* still being played at the end of the twenty-first century, it will undoubtedly be a vastly different game from the version now in existence. Conceivably, it will be a game played by people against computers—a game where, thanks to computerized dictionaries, kibbitzers, and Monday morning quarterbacks will be able to use IBM readouts to see what moves the contenders should have made in the world Scrabble Cup final.

With computers programmed to memorize every acceptable word in the English language, Scrabble players 100 years from now will be able to feed their racks' scrambled letters into the electronic brain and instantly get a printout showing all possible word combinations at their disposal. Not only will a properly programmed computer feed back all legal seven-letter board busters, but it will also be able to list every possible play down to two-letter words—and grade the words in point values. The encroachment of computers into the game may be abhorrent to Scrabble purists, but they would be wrong to scoff at the idea as "farfetched."

□

Lee Tiffany heads the subsidiary at Selchow & Righter that owns the Scrabble copyright in the United States, and he plans to use a computer to produce the ultimate Official Scrabble Players' Dictionary.

It was Tiffany who first started talking about using computers for move-by-move analysis of individual games. "Just imagine, with computer printouts of rack combinations, we can get lists of all acceptable words hidden in the jumbled racks, and then the guys with the photographic memories can memorize the lists. Then we'll really have something. The top players will be able to memorize Scrabble openings and plays the way professional chess players do."

Tiffany envisions the day when a world Scrabble championship garners as much attention as the Fischer-Spassky chess battle in Reykjavik, Iceland; regional and national play-offs; big purses for prize money; a system whereby Scrabble fanatics will be able to recreate move by move the champions' play on their own boards at home.

□

The first steps in that direction came several years ago when Tiffany and a few dedicated Scrabble players researched the idea of playing Scrabble competitively in tournaments. "I got interested and several other people got interested, "Tiffany said. "We had to see if there was any lasting interest in the game—not only in tournaments, but in the game itself. Remember it had been around for 25 years."

Tiffany said the one thing he didn't want was a fad—a hot-for-a-minute, then cold-forever tournament like jacks or hula hoop competitions from the fifties. "And I didn't want gimmicks like Scrabble marathons and underwater tournaments."

Tiffany soon discovered that there were thousands of people out there playing Scrabble in their Baltimore houses, New York apartments, and Miami holiday places just itching to get out and test their skills against other Scrabble aficionados. Thus Tournament Scrabble was born with a national players' organization, a players' handbook, new rules, a Scrabble newsletter, and even a Scrabble players' T-shirt with the words spelled out across the chest in tiles.

It was a version that Tiffany said would be the Scrabble of the future.

Alfred Butts, the man who invented the game, said he hated it.

□

The small, teaser advertisements started appearing in the book review pages of *The New York Times* around Christmas 1973. The one-inch-long spot ads invited Scrabble players to take part in the first-ever New York City Scrabble-off.

The tournament organizers expected a few hundred players to turn up, yet over 13 consecutive Sundays more than 2,300 players made the trek to the Brooklyn War Memorial hall in the shadow of the Brooklyn Bridge, to vie for one of the 12 finalists' berths.

To accommodate such a throng and to prevent fisticuffs, the organizers drew up the first of a series of new tournament rules, which, more and more, are becoming standard play in the United States. One of the most dramatic new rules was the use of a two-minute time limit, enforced that first year by a Rube Goldberg contraption that looked like an antique coffee grinder with a red clock hand on top, which took two minutes to move from the top to the bottom. It had to be rewound each turn and sounded distractingly like a coffee grinder as the time ground away. There was one on each table. When a player's two minutes were up, he had to have completed a word on the board or forfeit his turn.

Thus the clock became as deadly a weapon as a good vocabulary, and a good player could, chess-style, keep pushing his opponent up against the time barrier.

Inventor Butts, who has never played in a tournament and who never will, said, "That doesn't seem fair. It doesn't seem like fun any more, and I want to play for fun."

For the 1975 championships the time-per-turn was increased to three minutes, and the players, with a year's practice behind them, seemed more comfortable playing against the clock. They also had stopwatches instead of the distracting coffee-grinder timers.

The refined system was criticized strongly, though, by the eventual 1975 winner, Frank Kuehnrich. "Time has to be a factor," he said, "but the best tournament method would be to time games like chess. Each player gets a set time to complete his moves for a game, and it's up to him to decide whether to use it up by taking ten seconds for one turn or four minutes." (See the game *Stopwatch Scrabble* in the chapter on Scrabble variations.)

In tournament play, during the elimination rounds each competitor plays three games against three different opponents. His score for each game 'win or lose' goes up on the board and is totaled at the end of the day. The 10 players with the highest cumulative scores then go forward to the play-offs against other weekly winners. All previous scores are wiped out, and the players start another series against other play-off opponents.

When the field is whittled down to 12 finalists, the scoring system changes, with the top dozen players competing in an orgy of round-robin style games against each other. Playing two-person matches, the style of all tournament play, each finalist plays every other finalist to complete 11 games in two days.

If one player wins all 11 games, then he is immediately declared the winner; but if two players have the same won-lost record, say 9–2 or 8–3, then the points spread is taken into account, and that is where scoring differs from earlier rounds. "We changed the scoring for the finals," Tiffany said, "to try to make it as fair as possible."

What the organizers tried to guard against was a player who fluked several high-scoring games and came out with the highest cumulative score even though he may have won fewer actual games than another more consistent finalist.

The new tabulating system can best be described as "negative scoring": At the end of each game, the only thing taken into account, apart from who won or lost, is the winning or losing margin. Therefore, a player who wins his first game by 50 points and the second by 100 and loses the third by 20 has an aggregate of plus 130 points. A player who loses the first game by 50 points, loses the second by 100, and wins the third by 20 has an aggregate of minus 130.

This system gives added meaning to a victory in which a finalist thrashes his opponent by, say, 200 points. In effect, that constitutes a 400-point margin, boosting the winner's running total by 200 points and slashing 200 points from the account of the loser. As we found out at the 1975 finals, this new scoring system can turn the competition in a neck-and-neck race in which the champion is not decided until the last moves of the last game.

On a chilly March Sunday in 1975 the 12 New York finalists, nine men and three women, trooped into the Brooklyn War Memorial hall for the last five rounds of the championship. They had played the first six rounds of the finals the previous Sunday. Inside the hall a roped-off section ran down the center of the room, and six tables were set up inside the cordon. The only sounds were an occasional murmur from the players and the constant clicking of plastic tiles being stirred in blue velvet tile bags or being dropped into place on blue, revolving boards that had a raised grid pattern for the tiles and that were first designed for blind people.

The tournament tiles are a burgundy color with white lettering, not the normal pale blond wood ones with black lettering, because the players insist they are easier on the eye for marathon Scrabble sessions.

The sporadic murmurs and the sound of the tiles made the place sound a bit like a high-class casino such as the one at Monte Carlo. Tiptoeing around the room and acting as a sort of grand marshal was Joel Skolnick, a bearded cigar-chomping Scrabblenik from the New York Parks, Recreation and Cultural Affairs Administration, who was one of the prime organizers of the annual tournament. Skolnick likes to sign his name J O E L
    8 1 1 1.

In championship play there is a constant stream of challenges and for the 1975 finals a bank of judges sat at the top of the room armed with copies of *Funk & Wagnalls Standard College Dictionary*. Some of the attempted words were surprising. Either the players who laid them down couldn't spell or else, and this happens frequently, they gambled that their opponents couldn't. For example, one player tried to get away with *acurate*, another tried *beastial*, and a third put down *ouijie*. Some of the words that were challenged and were found in the dictionary included: *nove, chez, tivy, wonned, kips, mir, skited, tinners, laving, esparto, inquirer,* and *wavey*. One player, desperately trying to have a word approved, wrote alongside his challenged word "*yeg*, also look under *yegg*."

In tournament play, when a word is disputed, the person who played it writes it down on a piece of paper and raises his hand. One of a team of blue-coated attendants scurries up and takes the paper to a judge, who consults the dictionary and then puts a check mark in one of two boxes on the ballot. The boxes say "Acceptable" and "Not Acceptable." The judge's word is final, and there is no space on the paper for a description of what a disputed word means or purports to mean. In Scrabble you don't have to know what a word means. You only have to know that it is a word and that it is in the dictionary being used as the arbiter.

In Tournament Scrabble, if a player is challenged and the challenge is upheld, he removes the offending tiles and forfeits his turn. If the challenge is disallowed, the disputed word stays, the player's score is tallied, and the challenger loses his next turn. In regular Scrabble play, the standard version, there is no risk to the challenger. All that happens is that the person who played the disputed word retracts it if the challenge succeeds; then play goes on.

The finalists in the New York play-offs were obviously honed for competition. According to Tiffany, "one of the 12 finalists this year admitted that he never went to the toilet without taking a dictionary along." Tiffany said that another good Scrabble player, who made the 1974 finals, refused to play in the 1975 tournament because "he said he'd been busy at work and hadn't had time to train. He said he needed at least a month of training—just reading the dictionary and playing with anagrams to get into championship form."

The 1975 contest went right to the wire in a battle between a 31-year-old Manhattan bachelor, who, when asked what he did for a living, said, "I play games," and a 31-year-old woman from the Bronx, who worked for the New York Department of Social Services. Frank Kuehnrich, an intense left-hander, who plays and works at the Chess Center Game House in New York, went into the final game with a won-lost record of 8–2. Lucy Sacks was trailing with a 7–3 record. Strengthening Kuehnrich's position was the fact that under the negative scoring system he had a 10-game balance sheet of plus 518. Lucy Sacks was plus 365 for the 10 games. It was a scheduling freak that matched Kuehnrich against Sacks in the final game of the round robin, but it gave the tournament a dramatic ending.

Lucy Sacks needed to win to tie Kuehnrich with a won-lost record of

8–3 each. But she also needed a decisive victory to overtake him on the negative scoreboard. In fact, she needed to beat him by 77 points. A win by 77 would have lifted Lucy Sacks from plus 365 for 10 games to plus 442 for 11. It would have dropped Kuehnrich from plus 518 for 10 games to plus 441 for 11.

Lucy Sacks beat Kuehnrich, and even he thought she had won the title, but she beat him by only 75 points. A single *E* on a triple-letter square instead of a standard square anytime in 11 games would have given her two more points and meant the difference between victory and defeat. If Lucy had had one of the computers that Lee Tiffany dreams about, she'd have known in advance exactly what was needed.

The actual words in the final game of the 1975 championships, shown on Board No. 24, were not that exotic. You must remember, though, that both players were competing under great tension, had just finished four other games, and were also competing with the clock.

When the time ran out, all but four of the tiles had been used, and, given a few extra minutes, one of the finalists would have had time to unload his, or her, remaining tiles to go out. Only one phony word sneaked onto the board. It was the word *prex* (8 *L–O*). According to Funk & Wagnalls, the word *prexy* is permitted as slang for a college president, but when shortened to *prex*, it requires a period after it and is therefore illegal.

The word *wot* (*E* 3–5) is legal—and not as a slang expression for "I beg your pardon." It is, in fact, the present tense, first and third person singular, of *wit*. The word *od* (13 *I–J*) is one of those staple two-letter hooks that all good players have engraved in their mental vocab books, and *darky* (5 *J–N*) is a legitimate, albeit offensive, word.

Nix (played *O* 6–8) is okay as acceptable slang for "nothing" or as the verb "to forbid" or "to disagree with" and also as a "water sprite" in Germanic mythology. *Mel* (10 *J–L*) is an obscure word meaning "honey," and a *tapir* (*D* 4–8) is a South American mammal.

Since those first Scrabble tournaments, the practice of pitting Scrabble players against each other in public has spread quickly. Tournaments have been held in Baltimore, New York, Wilmington, Philadelphia, Miami, Oakland, Dallas, and Sacramento, with the list growing each year. They even held tournaments in the Catskills, but the New York resorts weren't the most conducive climates for applied competition. The organizers complained that several people decided the lure of the sun and the bars was too great, especially when they were trailing, and several games were never completed.

The spread of tournament play is one reason why Tiffany is keen for players to adopt tournament rules, which appear at the end of this chapter, even when playing at home. Another reason is that Scrabble has moved

BOARD NO. 24

	A	B	C	D	E	F	G	H	I	J	K	L	M	N	O
1						T₁								H₄	E₁
2					B₃	E₁			B₃				F₄	A₁	
3				W₄	E₁	E₁		V₄	A₁	N₁		L₁	I₁		
4			T₁	O₁	N₁		Q₁₀		N₁				A₁	R₁	
5			A₁	T₁			U₁		D₂	A₁	R₁	K₅	Y₄		
6			P₃		Z₁₀	O₁	O₁		I₁			I₁			N₁
7			I₁		O₁		T₁		T₁			E₁			I₁
8			R₁	A₁	N₁	T₁	E	R₁	S		P₃	R₁	E₁	X₈	
9		C₃			E₁	H₄				D₂	O₁		L₁		
10	C₃	L₁	O₁	U₁	D₂	Y₄			M₃	E₁	L₁		F₄		
11		A₁							E₁	W₄	E₁				
12		M₃	I₁	G₂				J₈	A₁		S₁				
13		S₁							O₁	D₂					
14				V₄	A₁	G₂	U₁	E₁							
15								S₁	I₁	N₁	G₂	E₁	R₁	S₁	

◩ DOUBLE LETTER SCORE

◩ TRIPLE LETTER SCORE

◻ DOUBLE WORD SCORE

▨ TRIPLE WORD SCORE

into the realm of bridge and chess, and members of the Scrabble Players organization will soon get "expert points" for every tournament win. They will also get expert points for victories in Scrabble clubs now being set up around the United States. The plan in late 1975 was for black expert points to be awarded for club victories, blue expert points for regional victories, and red points for national finals.

The breakdown of gradings for Scrabble players is as follows:

New Player
Intermediate
Master
Expert
Senior Expert
Advanced Senior Expert
Life Expert

Before a Scrabble club can be sanctioned and permitted to award Scrabble expert points, it must have a qualified club director, who must be over 21 years of age and who has passed an examination based on a club manual drawn up by the Scrabble Crossword Game Players, Inc. The cost of getting a club charter, sanctioned by the players organization, is $25. It costs $5 for the manual and the director's examination, $10 for the paper work and processing fee, and $10 for the annual licensing fee.

Scrabble clubs are fairly new to the game, and the players organization hopes to regulate all clubs and make sure that each club plays by Tournament Scrabble rules. The official players organization recognizes two types of clubs—open and closed. Closed clubs are nonprofit organizations for religious groups, colleges, senior citizens, and fraternal associations. Open clubs are profit-making affairs blessed by the Scrabble Crossword Game Players, Inc., after a club director has passed the club manual exam. Open clubs are restricted to the extent that players must be members of the national organization and each club must have a regular playing schedule for games so that visitors can be guaranteed a match. The national organization recommends a fee of $3 for an afternoon or an evening of club play with an absolute minimum of 50 cents a session for senior citizens. Scrabble Players, Inc. has also drawn up a special $9 package for schools to start junior clubs.

Another way you can get a good public game of Scrabble—and possibly be hustled out of some money as well—is to check out chess, checkers, and table-tennis clubs in your city. The official clubs frown on these Scrabble venues, and the ground rules for starting a club prohibit the playing of other games like chess and bridge in the same room or hall.

However, in places like New York, many game houses feature Scrabble along with chess, checkers, and backgammon; and these places are popular, even though a victory there does not make you eligible for Scrabble expert points. One of them, which is open 24 hours a day, is the Chess Center Game House, at 143 West Seventy-Second Street. If you go there, be careful—or be good: one of the men who works there is Frank Kuehnrich, the New York champion for 1975.

9 TOURNAMENT SCRABBLE RULES

The following are the rules adhered to by players in Scrabble tournaments. There are some variations on the standard rules, and the biggest difference is the time restriction of three minutes maximum per move.

1. To Start

a) There should be 100 tiles in the set. Both players should count them and place the tiles in the tile bag. In Tournament Scrabble a bag is always used. Tiles are never placed face down alongside the board as a pool as permitted in basic Scrabble.

b) Each player draws a tile to determine who gets the starting position. The player with the letter nearest the beginning of the alphabet has first move. A blank supersedes all other letters, and a player who draws a blank outranks a player who draws an A.

c) Both players must return the starting tile to the tile bag, which is then thoroughly shuffled by either or both players.

d) The player who has won the start fills his rack with seven tiles from the bag. The process is immediately repeated by his opponent, and the game begins.

2. The Clock

a) There are actually two clocks in Tournament Scrabble. The master clock, controlled by the tournament director, signals the beginning and end of each game and once started, runs uninterruptedly for sixty (60) minutes. The second clock is the three-minute timer on each table, which is controlled by the contestants and used to signal the length of each turn. The tournament director starts the main clock as soon as the players have returned their starting tile to the bag and *before* they draw their first rack of seven letters.

b) The official clock cannot be stopped during a tournament no matter what problems may occur in an individual game.

c) If a player must leave the table during a game, he loses as many turns as it takes for him to return. A game monitor sits in for him. The monitor is forbidden to touch the board or substitute as a player. He merely records "pass" on the score sheet each time the absent player's turn comes around and sits out the three-minute segments. The opponent continues to play.

d) The first player's three-minute timer is started as soon as both players have drawn their original seven tiles. The timer is then reset at the start of each turn throughout the game.

e) If a player plays a word before his three-minute limit has expired, he immediately announces his score, returns the timer to the start position, and the opponent starts his next turn. Each turn is a "clean slate," and a player cannot build up a time bank by demanding unused time from a previous turn when the clock expires on a later turn.

f) As soon as a player's time runs out his opponent must immediately notify him and from that second the player is prohibited from placing any further tiles on the board. Any player who has not placed a complete word on the board by the time his three-minute clock runs out must forfeit his turn. A pass is recorded on his score pad, and play reverts to his opponent.

3. The Dictionary

a) The *Funk & Wagnalls Standard College Dictionary* (1973 edition) is considered *the* word Bible for Scrabble tournaments. Any word found in this dictionary and labeled as a part of speech is permitted except for the following: capitalized words, prefixes and suffixes standing along, abbreviations, words requiring a hyphen, words requiring an apostrophe, and any word that is not labeled as a part of speech.

b) All foreign, archaic, colloquial, slang, obsolete, and italicized words are acceptable if found in Funk & Wagnalls and providing they are not outlawed by the preceding exceptions in rule 3a. The Funk & Wagnalls lexicographers determine when a foreign word becomes part of the English vocabulary. If a word is not in Funk & Wagnalls and does not meet the preceding conditions, it will be ruled unacceptable by the tournament judges. If a word appears in the dictionary as part of the definition of another word and is not listed itself, it is unacceptable.

c) Funk & Wagnall lists only the comparative (*er*) and the superlative (*est*) forms of one-syllable adjectives where there is a spelling modification—*dry, drier, driest*—or a complete change of form—*bad, worse, worst*. Other one-syllable adjectives that have standard comparative and superlative forms—*cold, colder, coldest*—are acceptable even though they are not listed in Funk & Wagnalls. Comparatives and superlatives of adjectives of two or more syllables will only be accepted if they are listed in the dictionary —*jolly, jollier, jolliest*.

d) Funk & Wagnalls only lists the declension of verbs and plurals of nouns when the transformation is unusual—*swim, swam, swum; goose, geese*. Normal declensions and plurals, although not listed, are acceptable—*walk, walking, walks, walked; dog, dogs*.

e) Letters of the alphabet have their own listing in Funk & Wagnalls. For example the letter *v* is listed as *vee*. When pluralized, it becomes *vees*. Letters of the alphabet, when spelled out like this, are acceptable. The letter *h* becomes *aitch*, and the letter *w* becomes *doubleyou*. Combinations such as *vs* and *ws* for plurals of the letters *v* and *w* are *not* acceptable. Foreign letters included in a dictionary's appendix under the category *alphabet* are not acceptable, but foreign letters (like Greek beta and omega) are acceptable when listed as separate entries.

f) No player may consult the dictionary during a game, and no other reading material is permitted at the game table. During any dispute, the tournament director and his staff will have sole access to dictionaries.

g) The tournament director is final arbiter in all dictionary disputes. His decision is not subject to appeal.

4. The Challenge

a) Once a player has completed his turn, his opponent may challenge any word, or words, that were formed on that play. He may not challenge a word in some other region of the board. In the original tournament rules, a player was entitled to challenge only one word formed by his opponent in the preceding turn. Now he may challenge any and all words formed in that turn.

b) To challenge, a player raises his hand and waits for a tournament monitor to come to the table.

c) The disputed word is written on a "challenge slip," a piece of paper on which the categories "Acceptable" and "Not Acceptable" are listed. The monitor takes the challenge slip to the judges, who consult the dictionary, make a ruling, and then relay the decision to the players.

d) If the challenged word is acceptable, the word remains on the board, the player receives full points for his turn, and the challenger forfeits a turn and enters the word "pass" on his score sheet.

e) If the disputed word is unacceptable to the judges, the player removes the offending tiles from the board, forfeits the points he would have scored from the play, and writes "pass" on his score sheet. He does not get a chance for another word.

f) The tournament director or his staff arbitrate on the validity of all disputed words.

5. The Play

a) The first player, if he chooses to take his turn, combines two or more tiles from his rack and places them on the board in either a horizontal or a vertical position to form a word. One tile must cover the pink square with a black star in the center of the board. For this he receives a double-word score. Diagonal words are prohibited.

b) He then counts his score for the turn, announces it aloud, and then enters it on his score sheet. Player No. 1 then draws as many fresh tiles as are necessary to bring his rack back up to the standard seven tiles. This procedure is followed after every turn.

c) Player No. 2 then adds one or more letters to those already on the board to form a new word or words. Like his predecessor, he must play his tiles on one row only and must play his word either horizontally or vertically. Any new words must touch at least one tile already on the board, and wherever fresh tiles touch previously played words or letters, those combinations must make complete, acceptable words. The player gets full credit for all words formed or modified in his play.

d) New words may be built by adding a letter or letters to a word already on the board; by placing a word at right angles to an existing word with the use of a letter on the board or by extending an existing word by one letter; or by placing a word parallel to an existing word, providing the adjoining words and letters form complete words, too.

e) Players are not permitted to shift tiles once a word is on the board. The tournament director is arbiter in such disputes.

6. The Blanks

a) There are two blanks in each Scrabble tile set, and they may be used to represent any letter a player desires. However, a blank must be designated as a specific letter as soon as it is played, and it retains that designation for the remainder of the game.

b) Whenever a blank is played, it is the opponent's responsibility to turn over the tile and to check that it is, in fact, a blank. If it is not a genuine blank, the player who used it must retract all his tiles for that move from the board and forfeit his turn. If a false blank is detected later in the game, it must remain on the board as an extra blank with no penalty to the player who used it.

7. Tile Selection

a) Whenever a player draws tiles from the bag in Tournament Scrabble, he must go through the following procedure. The newly selected tiles are placed face down on the table alongside the player's rack. He then checks to make sure he has drawn the correct number of replacement tiles to bring his rack back up to seven tiles. If he has drawn too many tiles, he informs his opponent, who then selects the excess at random from the upside-down tiles and returns the extras, sight unseen, to the tile bag.

8. Passing

a) Any player may use his turn to exchange any or all the letters in his rack for fresh tiles from the tile bag. He does this by drawing the unwanted tiles from his rack and placing them face down on the table alongside his rack. He next takes the same number of new tiles from the bag and places them face down on the table while he checks to make sure he has drawn the correct number of replacements. Then the new tiles are placed on the rack, and the discards, still face down, are returned to the tile bag, which is shuffled. That operation constitutes a complete turn, and any player who passes may not touch the board or play a word during his passing turn.

b) Any player may pass at any point in the game provided there are seven or more tiles in the tile bag. Further tile exchange is prohibited once that minimum has been reached.

c) It is not compulsory for a player to exchange tiles when passing. He may pass and retain the same seven tiles in his rack as part of play strategy. However, if both players pass for three successive turns, the game is terminated, and the player with the highest score wins.

9. The End

a) The game can end in one of three ways: The players can exhaust the tile supply, and one of them can go out; they can end the match by mutual consent if neither can place his final letters on the board; the tournament director's 60-minute time limit can expire.

b) The tournament director gives a six-minute warning signal as the end of the time period approaches. If a semicompleted word is on the board at the time of the final signal, no points are awarded for that turn. If a player has just finished placing a word on the board at the bell and there are tiles remaining in the tile bag, he must draw as many tiles as possible up to the standard seven.

10. Scoring

a) The score for each turn is compiled by adding the sum of the letter values for all words formed or modified during the play plus any additional points awarded from placing tiles on premium squares. The score value for each letter is stamped on the bottom right-hand corner of the tile. The blanks score zero.

b) Premium letter squares are counted as follows. The score of a *letter* is DOUBLED when it lands on a light blue double-letter square.

The score of a *letter* is TRIPLED when it lands on a dark blue triple-letter square.

c) Premium word squares are scored as follows. The score for the entire WORD is DOUBLED when one of its letters, including the blanks, lands on a light pink, double-word score square. The score for the entire WORD is TRIPLED when one of its letters, including the blanks, lands on a red triple-word score square. If a word covers two double-word squares, then the total score is DOUBLED and then REDOUBLED for FOUR times the face value of the word. If a word covers two triple-word squares, then the total score is TRIPLED and then RETRIPLED for NINE times the face value.

d) The premium letter squares and the premium word squares apply only in the turn in which they are first played. After that, letters covering premium squares count at face value only.

e) In the scoring of a turn, all premiums for double- and/or triple-letter squares must be included before doubling or tripling the complete word.

f) When two or more words are formed in the same play, each word is scored fully with the common letter being accounted for in each word. This applies to premium squares as well as to standard squares.

g) Any player who manages to use all seven of his tiles in a single turn receives a bonus of 50 points for his "bingo" word. It is added to his regular score for the turn after all premiums have been totaled.

h) After his turn, each player announces his score and fills it in on his score sheet. In Tournament Scrabble he also fills in a listing of all words formed on that play. Each score is checked by the opponent, and at the end of the game the score is checked and validated by the tournament director.

i) At game's end each player has his score reduced by the sum of all tiles remaining in his rack. If tiles are still left in the tile bag,they are ignored. If one player has gone out, his score is increased by double the total of his opponent's unplayed letters, and the other player's tally remains the same.

j) The player with the highest score wins the game.

k) In the event of a tie, the player with the best single word score in the game is declared the winner.

Part III

STRATEGY

10 THE START

If you play basic Scrabble, the start of each game is decided by pure luck: each player draws a sample tile from the bag, and the person with a letter closest to A wins the right to start the game.

There are only two rules controlling the start. The opener must use two or more letters in his opening word, and one of those letters must cover the star in the center of the board. For hitting that star, the first player doubles his score for the turn.

There are more exciting starts, involving mandatorily longer words, and these are listed further back in the book under Game Variations.

Alfred Butts experimented a lot on a starting position for his game and for a while favored the top left-hand corner. "I tried all kinds of things to try to get the best arrangement for the start," he said. "I went to the top left-hand corner of the board because when you make words, they run from left to right and from top to bottom. I tried a lot of things, but I have to admit that that one really didn't work as well," he said.

When Jim Brunot took over the game to market it, he rejected all ideas of a floating start and fixed the "go" square in the center of the board. He made the star pink—like the double-word squares that crisscross the board—and he guaranteed a bonus for the starting player.

He also, however, cunningly rearranged the double-letter premium squares that guard the center star, and if you have a close look at the board, you can see why the follow-up players often outscore the game opener despite his double-word bonus. By laying down any starting word of two letters, the kickoff player automatically exposes two double-letter scores—one above and one below his word or one on each side of his word.

If his word is three letters in length, he also exposes a triple-letter square. If it is four tiles in length, he exposes a double-word opportunity to the follow-up player. And if his opening word is five letters in length, a naïve starter can also become a pawn for the next player's raid on a triple-word score. A five-letter word run straight out from the center star goes dangerously close to a triple-word square. The next player can add an ending like -est or -ing to the opener's own word and profit handsomely.

So you can see the start is selfishly important apart from the fact that the opening round of play determines whether a game is going to be an open, freewheeling one or a complicated, two- and three-letter word war of attrition.

Many starting players feel they have no control over the board and merely drop their four-, five-, or six-letter word across the middle of the board. The only decision they make is whether to let the word run vertically or horizontally.

There are, however, several things the player with the opening position can do to protect his lead and get the most out of his first-down advantage. The first thing to remember is that this time is the only time in the whole game when you can play your hand with total freedom. Just this once you don't have to worry about other people's letters on the board blocking your way or stunting your word growth. The board is clean. It is empty. It is yours.

It shouldn't be necessary to point this out, but a lot of players seem to have a fetish for tidiness and symmetry when starting a game. If they are starting with a five-letter word, they place it neatly smack in the middle of the board with one letter covering the center star and two letters running out on either side. By doing this, they may be scoring imaginary points for neatness, but they are robbing themselves of points on the tally sheet. For example, on Board No. 25, I start with the word *march*. Placed in the middle of the board, it hits no double-letter squares and gives me a score of 12, which is doubled as the starter's bonus for a final 24. If however as on Board No. 26, I start off-center (from 8–*D* through 8–*H*), the letter *H* hits the center star rather than the middle *R*, and my score is better. The *M* covers a double-letter square, which will be quadrupled by the end of the turn, and the 24 points become 30. Automatically, I reshuffle the letters before playing the word *march*, but the alternative word *charm* doesn't improve my score; so I settle for the 30.

"Aha," says the alert student, "if you had played the word *march* vertically or horizontally and started from the center, the higher-value letter *H* would have landed on a double-letter square instead of the *M* and given you 2 more points, as in Board No. 27." The sacrifice of these 2 points is what I call insurance. A five-letter word like *march*, started from the center, takes you to within three tiles of a triple-word score. All the next player needs in order to go *marching* ahead of you are the tiles *I*, *N*, *G*, and he hits the triple-word square and scores 48 points. It is far better to settle for the lower opening score and keep the triple-word square at a decent distance.

□

BOARD NO. 25

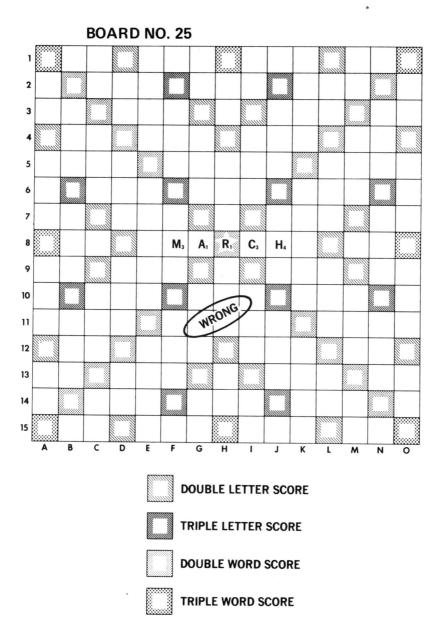

DOUBLE LETTER SCORE

TRIPLE LETTER SCORE

DOUBLE WORD SCORE

TRIPLE WORD SCORE

BOARD NO. 26

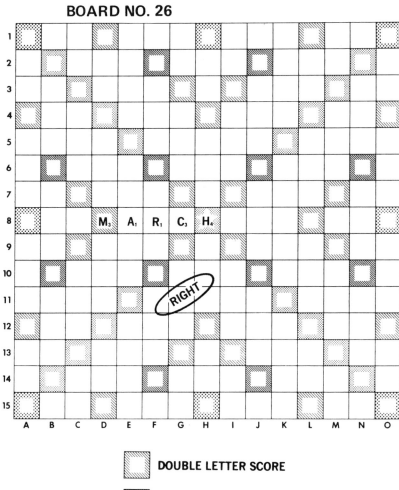

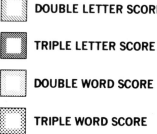

DOUBLE LETTER SCORE

TRIPLE LETTER SCORE

DOUBLE WORD SCORE

TRIPLE WORD SCORE

BOARD NO. 27

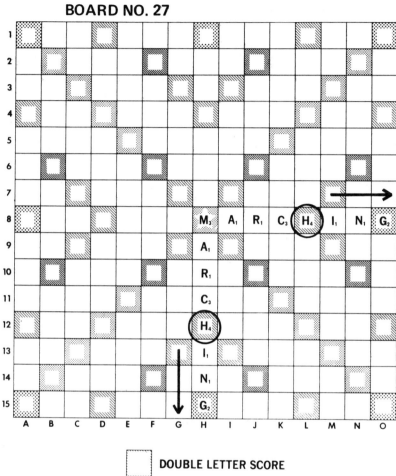

DOUBLE LETTER SCORE

TRIPLE LETTER SCORE

DOUBLE WORD SCORE

TRIPLE WORD SCORE

The importance of the opening placement of letters cannot be stressed too heavily. For example, in a lucky opening game recently, I had the letters R,X,M,T,E,E,E in my rack. We had agreed upon a five-letter word minimum to start, and after my opponent failed to open, I ran the word *extreme* down the board. I mention this play because it was a good example of how lucrative good letter placement can be, not only at the start, but throughout the game.

By centering the word, as on Board No. 28, I would have received 86 points (18 for the word, double for the start, 50 for the seven-letter bonus). By starting the word high and running it from squares H–3 through H–9, as on Board No. 29, I placed the high-scoring letter X on a double-letter square, giving it a total of 32 points of its own. The total score for the hand was 98 (24 for the word, double for the start, 50 for the bonus), an improvement of 12 points just from board management.

Also by starting high, I kept the word away from the bottom triple-word square. If I had started smack on the center star, the word would have carried to within one tile of the triple-score square (H–15), and an opponent would have needed only an S to make *extremes* and collect 51 points for lengthening my word, as on Board No. 30. Then if he added his own horizontal word, say *squaw*, worth 91 by itself, he would have had a total of 142 for the turn.

The score for the word *extreme* was high enough for me to break a starting rule: don't place vowels adjacent to the double-letter squares that surround the center star. I mentioned earlier Brunot's cunning positioning of these premium squares. If, on your opening play, you place a vowel in squares H–7 or H–9 on a vertical word or on squares 8–G or 8–I on a horizontal word (Board No. 31), you make it easy for the next player to place a high-scoring consonant on either side of your exposed vowel and thereby double the face value of each consonant. It is better, if possible without crippling your own word, to put a vowel on the center star and consonants on either side (Board No. 32) and increase the chance of your opponent's having to use low-scoring vowels on the double-letter squares. In the case of the word *extreme*, it was better to break the rule and collect the bonanza for the strategically placed letter X.

□

One final starting tip. If your first rack of tiles is just a string of vowels and low-value consonants and the most you can get from a five-letter word is 5 points, doubled to 10 for the starting bonus, then seriously consider throwing in some or all of your tiles and drawing a fresh set. A 10-point score from a word stocked with vowels is only going to open the floodgates for your opponent.

BOARD NO. 28

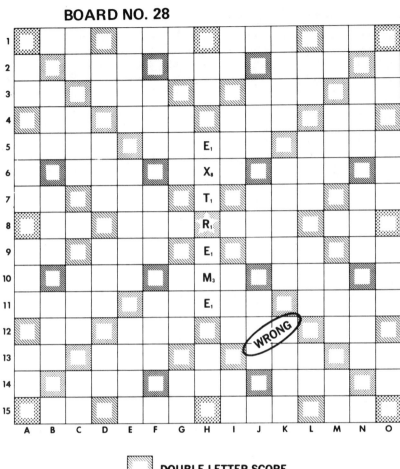

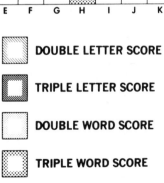

DOUBLE LETTER SCORE

TRIPLE LETTER SCORE

DOUBLE WORD SCORE

TRIPLE WORD SCORE

BOARD NO. 29

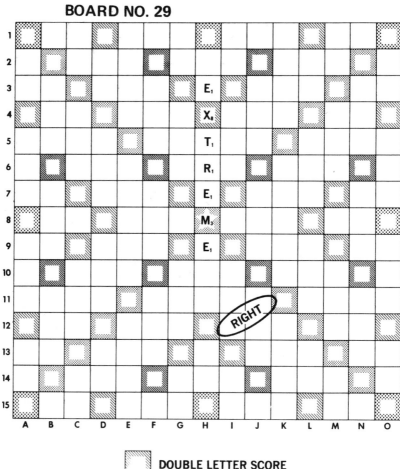

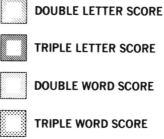

DOUBLE LETTER SCORE

TRIPLE LETTER SCORE

DOUBLE WORD SCORE

TRIPLE WORD SCORE

BOARD NO. 30

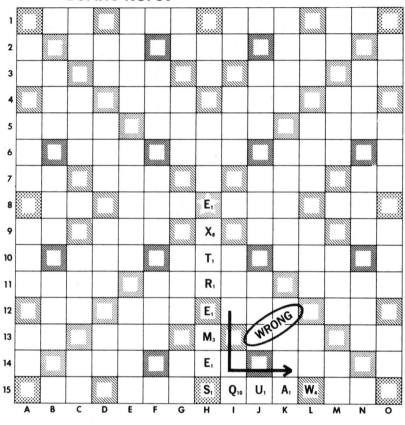

DOUBLE LETTER SCORE

TRIPLE LETTER SCORE

DOUBLE WORD SCORE

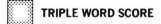
TRIPLE WORD SCORE

BOARD NO. 31

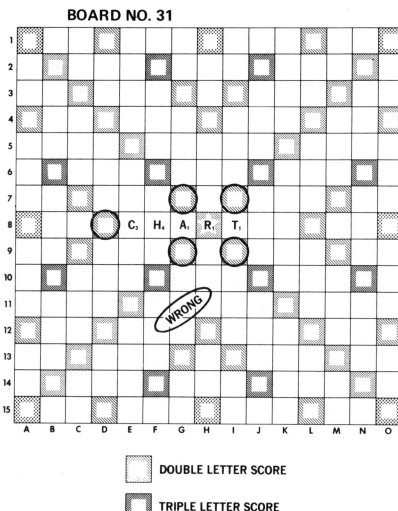

DOUBLE LETTER SCORE

TRIPLE LETTER SCORE

DOUBLE WORD SCORE

TRIPLE WORD SCORE

BOARD NO. 32

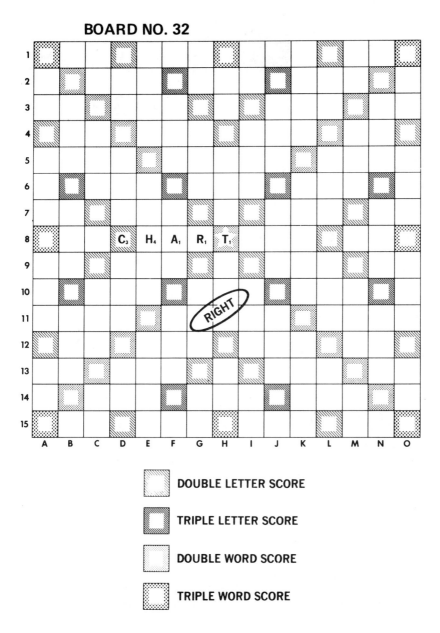

DOUBLE LETTER SCORE

TRIPLE LETTER SCORE

DOUBLE WORD SCORE

TRIPLE WORD SCORE

THE PLAY—FROM
TOP TO BOTTOM

By now it should be obvious, I hope, that there is more to this game of Scrabble than two people blithely dropping tiles on a patchwork board. It is true, as I have said before, that the sole object in Scrabble is to plant your tiles across the board more skillfully and with better results than your competitor. But there are numerous ways you can do that. You can, from the start, play offensively or defensively; you can try to outsprint your opponent, or you can try to grind him down like a marathon runner.

You can also, if you are in the mood, play an unpopular but often victorious game as a spoiler and tighten the noose on the game so effectively that it almost expires.

Sometimes the luck of the draw or your opponent's luck and/or skill will make you switch from an offensive style to a defensive style in mid-game. On the other hand, there are occasions when you are ahead by, say, 100 points and you feel like opening the board up and making a showy run for home. Be warned, though, that many games have been lost in the last few plays by smug leaders following that exact same course.

Whether you play conservatively or flamboyantly, openly or in a tightfisted manner, there are some absolute don'ts to remember. *Don't* open up a triple-word score square for your opponent. I'd like to say *never* do it, but there are exceptions, especially late in the game, when by doing it you get a decisive score of 50 to 70 and when all the high-scoring letters like the Z, Q, X, and J have safely gone.

Also try to keep your big tiles away from double-word squares (unless your word covers it anyway). After all, you've drawn the high-scoring tile, so you should be the only one to get the benefit from it. Obviously, there's nothing worse than playing a word like *zeal* and getting very little for it and having your opponent come along to extend it to *zealot* in a way that just happens to reach a double- or triple-word score, and he runs away from you.

□

Another cardinal rule when playing with someone adept at making seven-letter bingos is to try to thwart his openings. Play words, if you can,

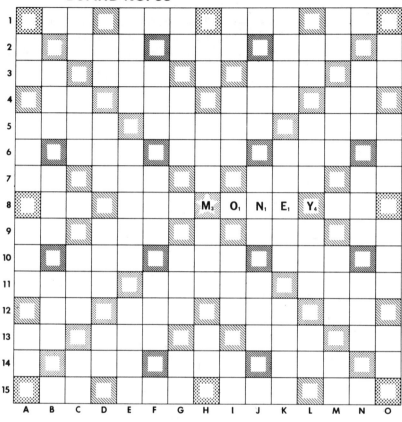

BOARD NO. 33

DOUBLE LETTER SCORE

TRIPLE LETTER SCORE

DOUBLE WORD SCORE

TRIPLE WORD SCORE

that are past tenses of verbs that he can't add an S to for an easy hook to a bingo word. Or keep putting small two- and three-letter word hurdles in his way so that he can't get a clear run at seven empty squares. These are things you have to keep an eye on from the very first moves, and it is the style of those very first moves that sets the tone of the game. For example, on Board No. 33, the first player puts down the word *money*, played horizontally 8 *H–L* to score 28 points. By that positioning he leaves double-letter squares exposed on either side of the *O*, but goes for that position to collect 16 points for the letter *Y* on a double-letter score, redoubled because it is the opening play.

The second player, in this hypothetical game, has drawn poor letters, including a couple of low-scoring *N*'s and a pair of *E*'s. If this occurs later in the game, he should pass all seven letters and start anew, especially if all his tiles have face values of one point. This is expanded on in the passing strategy section later in the book.

But this early in the game Player No. 2, already nearly 30 points behind, is not keen to forfeit a turn and perhaps fall 60 or 70 points behind. In addition, by passing, he is giving his opponent a second unencumbered attack on the board, and the letter *M* is in a position that conceivably could be run out for a seven-letter bingo and a triple-word score. The letter *Y* from the word *money* is also sitting out there as an inviting tail on a double-word score play.

Player No. 2 makes a play that serves two purposes. He unloads four letters in a move that is called "dumping" and therefore gets to replenish more than half of his rack without passing. And, more important, by a defensive placement he lassoes the board. The play he makes on Board No. 34 is to put down the word *none*, and to tie up the board, he glues it to the previous word and runs it right along under the *O.N.E.Y.* With that viselike move, he forms five words and scores 17 points. But, most important, he has used his low-scoring tiles to shut off the triple-word score threat and to foul up openings on several other lines and has managed to replace four of his tiles.

It is obvious that there were other moves available to him, but none unloaded as many tiles or so effectively blocked the board. In addition, with the same letters he could have been in trouble. If he had naïvely branched *none* or a similar word from the base word *money*, he would have given his opponent not one hook-letter, but a whole fisherman's hatful (Board No. 35).

□

There are some people who abhor such Scrabble strategy. Alfred Butts, Jim Brunot, and Australia's Tibor Urban are among them. They will

BOARD NO. 34

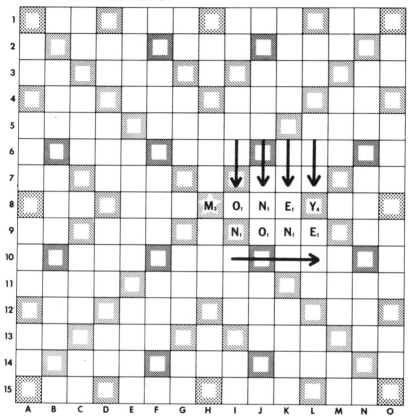

DOUBLE LETTER SCORE

TRIPLE LETTER SCORE

DOUBLE WORD SCORE

TRIPLE WORD SCORE

BOARD NO. 35

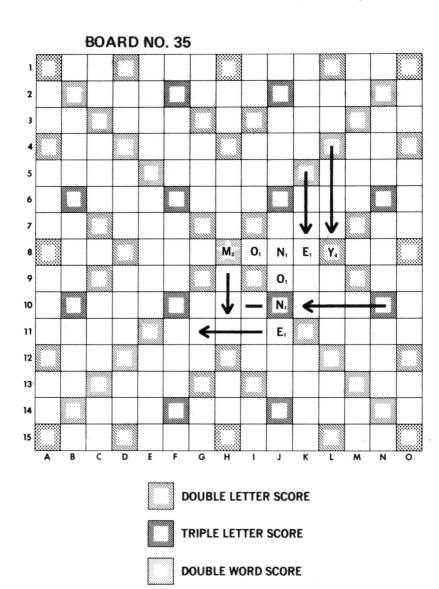

DOUBLE LETTER SCORE

TRIPLE LETTER SCORE

DOUBLE WORD SCORE

TRIPLE WORD SCORE

develop a board so wide open that you can drive a Panzer division across it and not hit a single tile. Brunot said, "I know there are a lot of players who like to play defensively and keep the game tight and that's all right with me. But I don't have to play that way. My wife and I played Scrabble right up to her death four years ago. We always enjoyed playing with an eye to the total score for the two of us rather than the difference of a few points between us. I still find that a more interesting approach to the game." Does he expose triple-word squares for an opponent? "Oh, yes. Frequently."

□

The temptation to play expansively is great, and I'll admit to having been guilty of it myself. One urge players often succumb to is to drop a particularly clever word, usually one of those tricky, albeit low-scoring, ones that people don't think you have in your vocabulary.

Sometimes it turns out to be worth less than if the player had made judicious use of a single *M* or a *Y*. You'd be surprised how many times the opportunity comes up in a game to put down a word like *my* or *em* or *ye* and land the *Y* on a triple-letter score. After all, with the smart use of a *Y*, it can be worth 24 points alone—12 going each way on a triple-letter square.

Which brings up the "x-plosion tactic." I think the letter *X* is my favorite letter in the bag, and as a two-letter zinger I have called on it many times to win a game. To me it is the most valuable letter of the big four because of the following quirk: There are no two-letter words using the *Z*. There are no two-letter words using the *Q*. There are only two two-letter words using the *J* (*ja* and *jo*, and *ja* is disputed in some dictionaries). That leaves the letter *X* worth 8 points before you even put it on the board.

It not only makes two-letter words when teamed with an *A* or an *E* or an *O*, but it also—and this is the kicker—makes a two-letter word when the letter *I* is placed after it. That means the letter *X* has the potential of being worth 48 points if you drop it on a triple-letter square and get something like *ox* going down and *ax* going across. You'd be surprised how many times a situation arises like the ones illustrated on Boards No. 36 and No. 37.

Throughout the game it pays to watch these chances like a hawk and to keep in mind words like *box*, *sox*, *pax*, *lox*, and *zax*. Near the end of the game it is even more important, defensively, to make sure you don't set up such gems. A person who can pick up 48 points with one letter in the dying stages of a game is obviously somebody to be reckoned with, and you should be alert for last minute "x-plosions."

BOARD NO. 36

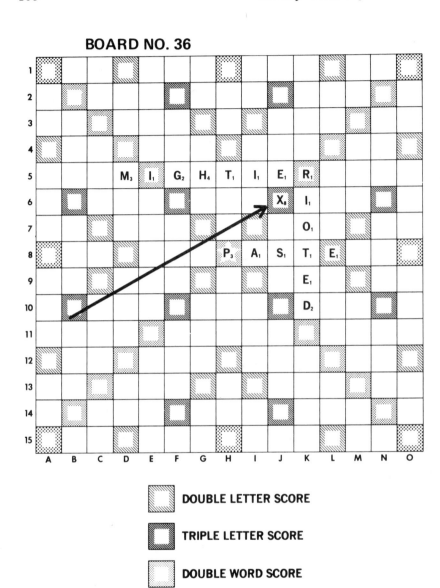

BOARD NO. 37

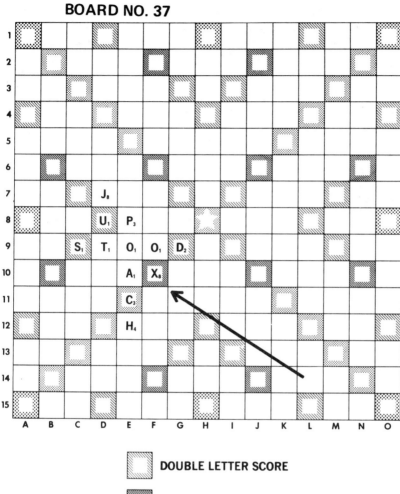

DOUBLE LETTER SCORE

TRIPLE LETTER SCORE

DOUBLE WORD SCORE

TRIPLE WORD SCORE

The same thing can be done at an effective, although less devastating, level with the letter *H*, which alone can be worth 24 points when teamed with vowels to make the words *ah, oh, eh, he, ho, ha,* and *hi*.

I mentioned the *Y* previously. It can be teamed in this two-way, triple-letter bonanza with four other letters to make the words *ay, by, my,* and *ye*. Besides being good scoring combinations, these letters also help tighten the board.

Sometimes two defensive players get into a Scrabble tussle that is something akin to "Indian Wrestling." Each exerts more and more pressure on the opponent by tightening the board, play by play, until it becomes a contest to see who submits first and breaks the board open again.

The example on Board No. 38 is not a very high-scoring one, but it does show how, turn after turn, the game stays tight until the area under attack is almost a solid block of tiles. There are eight moves in that small interlocking block, and unraveling them is like trying to undo one of those Chinese wood puzzles. It starts with the word *mate* (8 G–J).

Using the letter and number code to track them, the other moves are as follows:

Move No. 2—*aye* (7 I–K); also makes words *at* (I 7–8) and *ye* (J 7 8)

Move No. 3—*bar* (6 I–K); also makes words *bat* (I 6–8), *aye* (J 6–8), and *re* (K 6–7)

Move No. 4—*red* (K 6–8); also makes word *mated* (8 G–K)

Move No. 5—*payee* (J 5–9)

Move No. 6—*aired* (K 4–8); also makes word *pi* (5 J–K)

Move No. 7—*ten* (L 4–6); also makes words *at* (4 K–L), *pie* (5 J–L), and *barn* (6 I–L)

Move No. 8—*bath* (I 6–9); also makes word *he* (9 I–J).

Play like that leaves the rest of the board looking naked, and now is as good a time as any to point out that even when you are playing the most open, free-flowing game imaginable, you still finish the game with less than half the Scrabble board covered. There are 225 squares on a Scrabble board, and only 100 tiles, including the two blanks.

□

To play a tight game it is imperative that you know at least some of the tricky two-letter words that are legal—words like *xi, ut, ka, na, em,* and *en*. There are around 70 of them listed in most dictionaries, and a list of the generally accepted ones are in the vocabulary section of this book.

It also pays, offensively or defensively, to have a good repertoire of

BOARD NO. 38

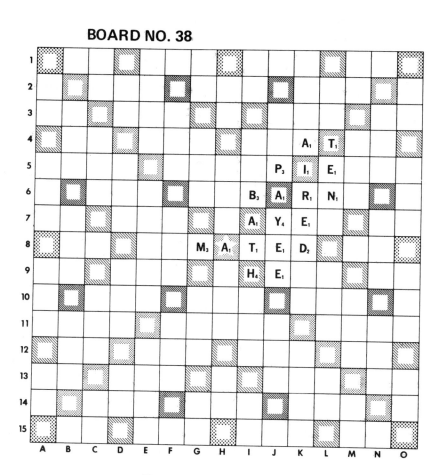

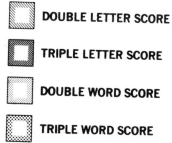

DOUBLE LETTER SCORE

TRIPLE LETTER SCORE

DOUBLE WORD SCORE

TRIPLE WORD SCORE

tricky three-letter words like *mho, haj, piu, rax, zax, ays,* and *phi*. These are also listed in the vocabulary section of the book.

□

Many good Scrabble plays are made by using the original word on the board and merely extending it to change its tense or inflection. For that reason, it is imperative to be always on the lookout for the option of adding *-ed, -ing, -iest, -er,* or *-es* to an opponent's word.

You should also keep in mind the option of transforming a word by the use of prefixes like *inter-, re-, mis-,* and *un-,* or by the addition of suffixes like *-ment, -ly, -able, -ness,* or *-er*. This habit of top-and-tailing words is even more important when you are drawing a seemingly endless supply of low-value tiles while your opponent keeps sucking up the big ones.

The experts say that luck has only a 12 percent influence on the game, and it is true that a skillful player with poor tiles will often beat a lesser player who has drawn the greatest tiles in the set. However that is slight consolation when you seem to have nothing but a roll call of one-point tiles on your rack.

The thing to do in such cases is to become proficient at word-bending—not only with the conjugation of verbs on the board or the declensions of nouns and adjectives, but by taking a word already on the board and by succinct addition of one or two tiles of your own reap a harvest.

After a short time, some plays become obvious, such as expanding *zoo* into *zoon, jet* into *jets* or *jetted,* and *qua* into *aqua.* But you can also get words like *kazoo* out of *zoo* and *jetty* and *jettison* from *jet* and *squat* and *quare* from *qua. Raze* can become *brazen, tamped* can be turned into a *stampede,* and so on. The big thing to remember is not to get discouraged if an opponent gets a word like *quiz* as on Board No. 39. There are oodles of retaliatory moves. A blank and an *ed* can give you *quizzed,* and you've got a double-word score that includes your opponent's Z and the previously played Q. It's as if those high-scoring letters had been in your own hand for that turn.

Take another example (Board No. 40). You jump on either end of the word *quip* and make it *equipment.* Once again, you are not only utilizing a Q already on the board, but you have also hit a double-word score.

The point to remember is that a good player can often make more from a high-scoring letter than the player who originally drew it from the tile bag and put it on the board. On Board No. 39, Player No. 1 received 22 points for *quiz* (an admittedly poor play because, despite capitalizing on the Q it did not land the Z on a premium square). When the word was

BOARD NO. 39

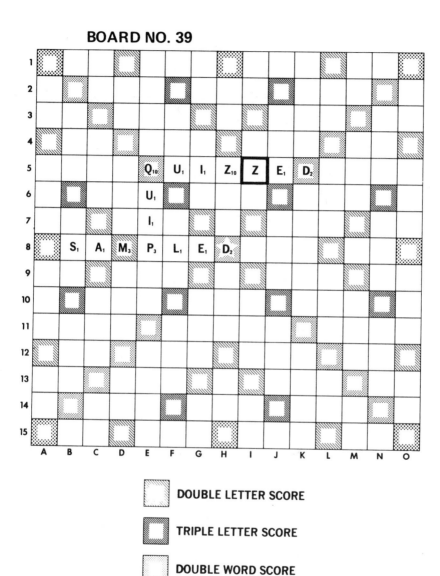

DOUBLE LETTER SCORE

TRIPLE LETTER SCORE

DOUBLE WORD SCORE

TRIPLE WORD SCORE

BOARD NO. 40

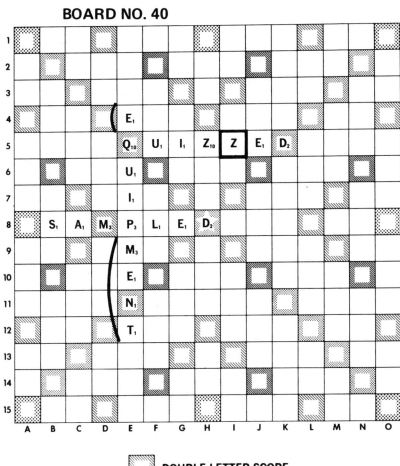

extended to *quizzed*, it was worth 50 points. On Board No. 40, *quip*, with a double-word count, was worth 30 points; extended to hit another double-word square, it was worth 44 points.

Such extensions are more common when both players are involved in a wide-open, offensive game, and they are a great leg up when you are at full stretch attempting to reach the high-scoring double- and triple-word score squares.

On Board No. 41, the clever use of the exposed, innocuous word *tie* gives a player the word *mightiest* for the capture of two double-word score squares—what I call a "double whammy." For this, the player gets 30 points (15 doubled) plus another 30 when the score is redoubled.

Double-doubles are uncommon, and triple-triples ("triple whammies") are rare, but they produce the highest scores on record for Scrabble freaks. The reason is that first Butts and then Brunot ordained that each player have seven tiles in his hand and then placed the triple-word squares *eight* spaces apart. To reach them, you have to have somebody's previously played tile as a stepping stone. It is only through these triple-triple plays, though, that you can get such mind-boggling scores as 200–350 in a single turn.

The record for a single word in the Butts's household is held by Nina Butts, who ran the word *quixotic* down the top right-hand side of the board. She leapfrogged over the word *fox*, already played by her husband, and finished up with a score of 284 for the turn. Unfortunately for Mrs. Butts, it was the X that was already in place covering a double-letter score. If the X had been hers and some other single-value letter had been on the line as the stepping stone, she could have scored 356 for the word, including the bingo bonus of 50.

□

You should guard against putting the stones in place for such moves. Even though they are rare, "triple whammies" do happen; and when they do, they can "whammy" you right out of the game. Never, never, never play a word like *raft* on Board No. 42, where your opponent can easily pick up one triple-letter score and without too much of a strain can reach across for a second. This obsession with double-doubles and triple-triples brings up a good, early-in-the-game strategy that I call the "Big H and Little H ploy."

If you look at Board No. 43, you will see that just outside the core of the board are strategically placed double-word score squares that form the outline of the letter *H*. There are two of these designs, the "Big H" and the "Little H." The "Big H" is outlined by double-word squares at *D*–4 and *D*–12, *L*–4 and *L*–12. The "Little H" is outlined by double-word squares

BOARD NO. 41

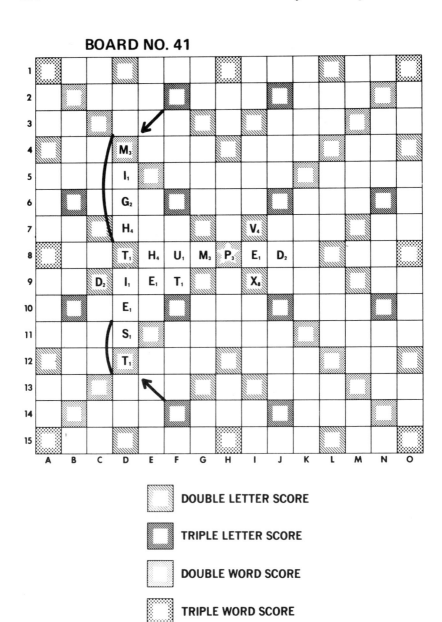

DOUBLE LETTER SCORE

TRIPLE LETTER SCORE

DOUBLE WORD SCORE

TRIPLE WORD SCORE

BOARD NO. 42

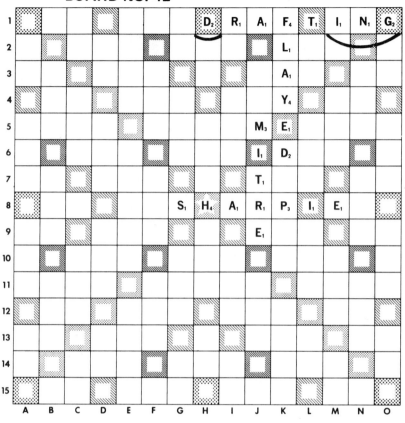

DOUBLE LETTER SCORE

TRIPLE LETTER SCORE

DOUBLE WORD SCORE

TRIPLE WORD SCORE

BOARD NO. 43

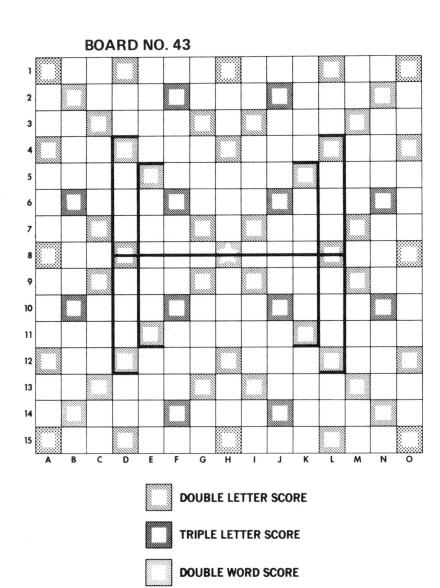

DOUBLE LETTER SCORE

TRIPLE LETTER SCORE

DOUBLE WORD SCORE

TRIPLE WORD SCORE

at *E*–5 and *E*–11, *K*–5 and *K*–11. The crossbar for each letter *H* is the horizontal middle line with the starting square's star in the center.

You can get from one pink square in the "Little H" to the other with no help from your opponent because they are within reach of each other—although a maximum seven tiles apart. However, if early in the game, and hopefully on his first move, your opponent makes that crossbar wide enough with a long, horizontal word, you need only six of your letters to go up three squares to the top of the goalpost and down three to the bottom to collect your "double whammy."

The fact that this is not achieved more often is because most shrewd starting players are conscious of such consequences and also because early in the game the area around the starting star is turbulent, unlike the eye of a hurricane. You'll usually find the region so littered that you can't get a clear run at both the top and the tail. To score on the "Big H," you need some assistance because the two double-word squares are nine spaces apart, and you only have seven tiles.

Obviously, this assistance from an obliging opponent is not going to come your way often, but you'll be surprised how many times it does once you know about this ploy and once you start to envisage two *H*'s branded on the board.

12 BINGOS

In the past few pages I have escalated from talking about two- and three-letter words to seven-, eight-, and nine-letter words stretching across the board.

It's time to talk about bingos.

The seven-letter bingo is to Scrabble what a hole-in-one is to a golfer. It's dramatic, it's gratifying, it's highly rewarding, and it can wreck an opponent's morale—especially if you can dish them up to him back to back.

The only time I ever won a Scrabble game by concession was when my opponent quit after I drew charmed tiles and scored three bingos and two triple-word score plays in my first five moves. Apart from your actual score, using all seven tiles in your rack in one move is worth 50 bonus points, which meant in the game I just mentioned that I had 150 points before I really started counting.

The idea of a 50-point bonus for a seven-letter play was not in the rules of Scrabble as drawn up by Alfred Butts when the game was still called Criss-crosswords. It was a fillip added by Jim Brunot when he took over the game, and it has proved to be one of the most exciting things in Scrabble. Apart from the obvious incentive for players to hunt through their tiles for seven-letter combinations, it has also given encouragement to players trapped with low-scoring tiles in their racks. A lot of bingos are scored by players whose seven tiles have a total face value of around 10 or 12. The bonus 50 gives added muscle to the score for that turn.

Anybody can, and should, score bingos, and I believe an average player should ring one up every game. Somehow, though, bingos (or "scrabbles" as they are sometimes called in England) elude people for years.

When I was in Australia doing some research for this book, I interviewed Tibor Urban, the man who owns the Scrabble name in Australia and manufactures the game there. He told me the wrenching story of one elderly couple who had been playing bingoless Scrabble for years. "They are old friends of mine, they're both about 80, and they have been playing Scrabble every day for 18 or 19 years. One day we were talking about laying down all seven tiles in one move. The wife told me that she'd heard about it but didn't believe it could be done. She said they had been playing all those years and not once had either of them put down all seven letters in one move."

The couple challenged Urban to a game. On his first move he spread out a seven-letter word.

□

It is true that some people are more adept at unscrambling anagrams than others and are also geared more closely to exploiting letters already on the board that can be built upon for bingo breaks. Some players, especially tournament competitors, have six-letter "key words" that they use as tools in building bingos. I call it the "satire syndrome" because one of those keys is the word *satire*.

This practice started a couple of years ago when somebody stumbled across the fact that the six letters comprising the word *satire* can be jumbled and scrambled with practically any other letter of the alphabet to make a seven-letter word. For the record, 18 of the 26 letters of the alphabet can be added to the letters in the word *satire* and can be transformed into at least 50 seven-letter words.

There are other popular key words like that (including *retina* and *santer*), and a list of all the possible combinations from these trunks is included in the vocabulary section at the back of the book.

It is fairly predictable that any bingo you get is going to include a lot of vowels. There are two reasons for this. First, although there are only five vowels and 21 consonants in the alphabet, the vowels account for 42 of the 100 tiles in the Scrabble set. The figure rises to 44 when the *Y* is used as a vowel. Second, the most common form of bingo occurs when you add three or four letters to the front of such word endings as *-ies*, *-ied*, *-iest*, *-ing*. Other recurring bingo endings are *-ion*, *-tion*, *-tian*, *-cing*, *-able*, *-ment*. When these letter combinations fall into your rack, make sure you recognize them, separate them, and try to sort your remaining letters into a bingo word.

Once you have a word, there's the problem of finding a place on the board to put it. A good opponent will at all times try to limit the exposure of "hooks" onto which you can attach your bingo. The easiest place to drop a seven-letter word is to plug it into an exposed S; so while you are building seven-letter words in your rack, it pays to lean toward words that pluralize easily with the standard S ending.

On the same plane, it also pays not to be complacent. Don't stop searching your hand for alternatives once a seven-letter word has materialized. For example, you have the letters *S,E,C,P,E,R,T* in your hand. They spell the word *respect*, and a lot of people, in the flush of success at building a bingo word, hunt no further. However, that same letter combination can be twisted to make the words *spectre* and *scepter*, and by making that additional effort to find extra words you often discover that a higher-scoring letter, like the *P*, lands on a triple-letter square for nine points rather than a tile with a face value of one.

Also, by having these alternatives in your head, you'll find it much easier to find a trunk word on the board on which to hang your seven-letter play. (This habit of automatically reshuffling a completed word to check out alternatives should also be applied to shorter words, and a list of good "switch-hitters" are listed in the vocabulary section.)

□

The two best tiles for bingos are the same ones that are regarded as the blue chips in other categories of the game. They are the letter *S* and the blank. The *S* is the most obliging letter in the game except for the chameleonlike blank, whether it be in your hand or on the table. If your opponent has left an exposed *S*, you can easily pin a bingo right on it; and if he hasn't and you have one in your hand, you can usually find somewhere on the board a word that is just begging to be pluralized, as on Board No. 44. Then you not only get your bingo down, with its 50-point bonus, but you also get to tag on the face value of the word already on the board.

You'd be amazed what words can be pluralized—virtually any noun and, in some dictionaries, virtually any word. This often disputed theory is explained in detail in the vocabulary section.

The blank, as I said, is Scrabble's chameleon. It's a wild card, a joker, a free ticket, and nowhere is it more effective than in a bingo word. After a few games, you realize why, when passing tiles back into the bag, you never pass an *S* or a blank. Some good bingo players follow an axiom that they never play the blank *except* as part of a bingo word. (The only exception is when they draw the *Q*, and all the *U* tiles are already on the board.) This is an extreme rule, unless you are a topflight player, but it is good policy to milk the blank for all it is worth and never ever to regard it as a filler.

Some players, I have noticed, fall to pieces when they draw the blank. It's almost as if they can't cope with the freedom of having a tile to which they can attach whatever designation they choose. And I have often seen players, good players, totally come apart when they have been blessed with two blanks at the same time. The major problem, and this applies to most bingo opportunities, is that players get locked into regarding the blank in limited terms. To them it is an extra *S* or, if they have the letters

BOARD NO. 44

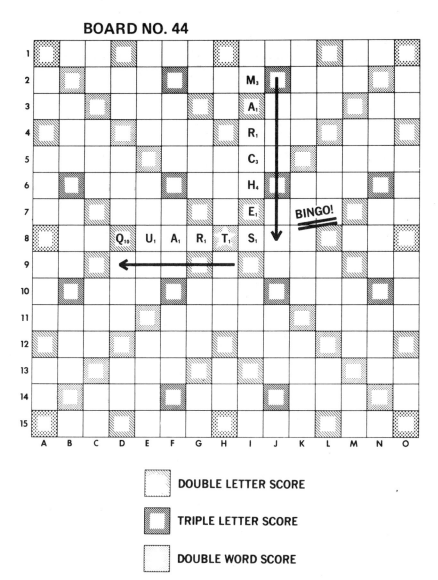

DOUBLE LETTER SCORE

TRIPLE LETTER SCORE

DOUBLE WORD SCORE

TRIPLE WORD SCORE

I,*N* in their rack, it automatically becomes a *G*. If they are holding an *R* or a *D*, the blank quickly becomes an *E* to make endings of *er* and *ed*.

These players limit their scope of bingos by not being adventurous enough, by not letting their minds picture the blank as any letter in the alphabet—even the *Z* and the *X* and the *Q*. Here's an example. In a recent game I was lucky enough to have a blank in hand along with the letters *R*,*B*,*A*,*E*,*I*,*N*. I developed them into the bingo word *brained* (using the blank as a *D*). This past tense verb was hard to place on the board—you can't pin the word *brained* onto an exposed *S*. By consciously bleaching the proxy *D* from my mind and letting the blank float pure and light, it was only a matter of time before several other bingo words came up. The ultimate word was *bearing*, with the blank substituting for a *G*, and I managed to run it up the board off an *S* to hit a triple-word score.

Often the blank will become five or six different letters, in your head, that is, until you finally hit on something worthwhile. Another example: For some reason, I have trouble with the letter *C*. I dislike drawing it and try to dispose of it as quickly as I can. The letter *V* is not one of my favorites either. In one recent game, though, I drew the *C* with the letters *E*,*L*,*I*,*A*,*R* and a blank. By letting the blank float, I came up with *reclaim* (using it as an *M*), *glacier* (using it as a *G*), and *reliance* (using it as an *E*), with an *N* already on the board.

□

I mentioned good word endings to help in making bingos, but when you are hunting for seven-letter giants, you should also keep in mind other good letter combinations like *th*, *ch*, *ph*, and *ght*. It's a bit like building a prefabricated house—the more pieces you have precut and presized, the easier it is to build, especially if the pieces are as compatible in the basement as they are in the first-floor bedroom.

□

By now you are probably all fired up to get into a game and drop five or six consecutive bingos. You should first read the following words of warning: Bingos are like hard drugs. Get a taste for them, and they can destroy you. I have become so obsessed by bingo-hunting in a game that I have lost by more than 100 points.

It happens like this. You have letters in your hand that you just know are a mere trifle away from a 50-point bonus. The word just won't come; so you play away a couple of the letters—the ones you think are contaminating your rack and preventing the bingo. You hope the next letters you draw will make an easier bingo opportunity. Worse still, you pass and toss back one or two letters and draw anew in the dangerous game of "fishing." (When that works, it's magnificent. When it fails, it is horrendous. It is exactly like trying to fill an "inside straight" in poker.)

Without your knowing it or even consciously agreeing to it, you are now totally committed to making a seven-letter word. While jockeying for position, you are falling behind, and suddenly it's a vicious circle. The more you hunt for a bingo ... the further you fall behind ... the more imperative it becomes that you make a bingo ... and the further you fall behind.

Finally, you get it. Jackpot. You collect your score and your 50-point bonus and discover that, after all the sweat and all those convolutions, your 80 points did not even make up the ground you lost over the preceding turns when you were bingo-hunting and your opponent was romping over a virtually undefended board.

I have been guilty of deliberately squandering four turns for a grand total of 22 points because of a Machiavellian plot to set up and capitalize on a "brilliant" bingo. I put this in print in the hope that never again will I be tempted to repeat it.

There are two simple reasons why this bingo strategy is fraught with hazards. One is that the obsessed bingo-hunter ends up playing against himself. Suddenly, consumed by bingoitis, he ceases playing his opponent, and his inspection of the board becomes cursory. He is engrossed in a one-man bubble, just himself and his rack. It degenerates into a tussle between those prenicious tiles and his mind. The tiles often win.

The second reason that this sort of nonsense often fails is because the opponent knows immediately what you are doing. He doesn't have to be overly observant to realize something strange is going on when a player who has been methodically scoring 35, 45, or 55 points in a turn suddenly puts down tiles that score 9, 6, and 7. The man has "bingo-hunter" written all over him. Forewarned, the opponent picks away at the board, nailing letters like *W* and *Y* and *F* to triple-letter squares while making sure that each move tightens the board and that no move exposes an easy bingo hook. As mentioned earlier, he can play words like past tenses of verbs ending in *ed* that cannot be pluralized, and he can also adroitly play words with letters like *C* and *V* in them.

These two letters (along with the *Z* and the *Q*) are the best defensive tiles in the pack. The reason is that there are no two-letter words starting with a *C* or a *V*, and there are no two-letter words ending in a *C* or a *V*. This is why you will often see a lone *C* tile holding back the tide as one-half of the board fills and the other half remains clear. I mentioned the *Z* and *Q* as being good defensive tiles because they, too, are immune from extension by adding a tile to make a two-letter word. However, these tiles carry such high face values that they are rarely used as blocking weapons.

□

One final thing to remember with bingos is that they are something like the elusive pot of gold at the end of the rainbow. Everybody knows they are there, but there are a thousand people who see or think they see a rainbow for every one who gets a piece of the gold. In this case, the gold is the 50-point bonus. But to put it in perspective, you should keep in mind that although a bingo is worth 50 points for all seven letters, a single X can be worth 48 when played properly. That's only 2 points less, you've used six fewer letters, and you've also kept your ulcer quiet.

13 RACK MANAGEMENT

Throughout this section on Scrabble strategy, I have detailed how to score with such-and-such a tile or how to score with a so-and-so combination. About now I can hear an exasperated chorus of "okay for you to talk ... you should see the tiles I get."

It may come as a shock to some self-pitiers, but the tiles you end up with in your rack are often your own fault. The rack that says I–I–I or the one that looks like a train whistle going T–O–O–O–T has often been assembled through the player's own recklessness, stupidity, naïveté, or a combination of all three.

It is true that you cannot be held responsible if you dip your hand in the tile bag and draw four tiles with the letter A on them and three with the letter I. You are guilty of a Scrabble offense, though, if you hold on to them through the next turn. You should sacrifice a turn and pass them back into the bag.

And you are also guilty if time and again you seem to end up with a rack full of vowels or seven straight consonants. There is a knack to keeping your tiles evenly seeded with vowels and consonants, and it is known to good players as "rack balancing."

□

The process of rack balancing is precisely what the name implies: keeping your rack equally balanced with vowels and consonants because it is a rare word indeed that doesn't have a reasonable mix of both categories of letters. Ideally, you should try to keep a near equal mix of vowels and consonants in your rack at all times to give you maximum flexibility in word-building.

Good practice for this is to play Inventor Butts's favorite Scrabble variation called "Double Bag Scrabble," in which the vowels and consonants are kept in separate bags. That means every single turn, when you go go replenish your rack, you have to make the decision as to whether your need for vowels is greater than your need for consonants.

Butts, who at one time unsuccessfully tried to convince Jim Brunot to have the tiles for vowels and consonants dyed different colors, noted that initially human greed gets the better of most players and they call heavily on the consonant bag. They end up with an impotent rack full of high-value, impressive-looking, but unplayable consonants.

The cardinal rule in rack management is this. Don't play every hand as though it were your last. If you have the letters W,H,Y,I,O,U,E in your rack, don't play the word *why*. It may be the highest score available, but you'll be stripping your rack of consonants and leaving yourself open and vulnerable. You may find that at best it is impossible to form a good word on the next turn and you'll have to pass, or worse you'll have nothing with which to defend the board if the need arises. It is better in that play to make the word *you* or *hey* or even *hi* or *wo* and suffer the lesser score until you can regroup.

Similarly, if your hand has five consonants and two vowels in it, don't play away the two vowels in a single turn. Keep one for insurance. For example, in your rack you have the tiles E,A,W,H,Y,P,T. You could unload four tiles in words such as *heap* or *hate* or *path*, but that would leave you devoid of vowels. A far better move would be to play the word *paw*. It not only leaves a vowel in the residue, but also shapes your hand for a possible bingo in the next turn.

This advance planning on bingos may seem ambitious, but it is a sound tactic to use, and good bingo players are endlessly trying to mold their racks into bingo springboards.

By playing the word *heap* the sample hand was left with the tiles W,Y,T. This wasn't as bad as it could have been because the Y often saves a vowelless hand. But by sacrificing a few points and playing *paw*, the player's residue consisted of the tiles E,T,H,Y, which are good bingo starters—*th* being a good combination as well as *ty* and *thy*.

□

Another thing to watch for when attempting to maintain a well-balanced rack is the duplication of letters. Obviously, this will happen. You'll dive your hand into the tile bag in quest of two vowels, and you'll come up with two tiles each marked L. The thing to do in this case is to make sure you play one of those duplicated letters in your next turn.

Some people have the mistaken idea that your odds are somehow better for forming high-scoring words, especially bingos, if you have more than one of a kind in your rack. Perhaps it's a mind-fooler that if you only have to keep five or six different letters in your head, you can make a word more easily. It's not true. This isn't poker, and pairs you don't need. If you have a rack of tiles that includes two L's and, say, two O's, then obviously your range of word possibilities is gravely restricted.

As soon as you draw a duplicate letter, you must plot to unload it in your next turn. As long as duplications remain in your hand, your chances of bingos are diminished, and you are playing under an unnecessary handicap. There are only two exceptions to this rule. One is when you have more than one S in your hand, and the other is when you have both blank tiles. With that assistance, you should be able to play away all seven tiles in your next turn. A further hindrance when you have two of a kind in your rack is the crippling, but not uncommon, experience of drawing a third identical letter. When that happens, you are well up the street you don't talk about.

Some people follow house rules whereby if a player draws more than two of the same letter, he can reject all duplicates (over two) and redraw without penalty. (See the chapter on game variations.) My attitude is that if a person is caught with three of a kind, that's his problem, and he can try either to play them away or, more sensibly, forfeit a turn and attempt to recycle the offending letters when his next turn comes around. Usually, it is suicidal to try to hold grimly on and play away three or four tiles of the same letter. Often you fall much further behind than if you elect to "take your lumps," miss one turn, and get rid of them all in one spring-clean.

If you do elect to play your way out of trouble, it pays to be well-stocked with good dumping words—especially ones that are full of low-value, duplicated vowels. Some of them have become stock dumping ground items in Scrabble. They are words like: *aalii, voodoo, eerie, luau, miaou, cooee, adieu, oleo, audio, iota, queue, bureau, apogee, hoodoo, peewee, fiancée, radii, ratio, ovaria*. There is a list of more than 50 good ones in the vocabulary section.

□

Another thing to keep in mind when you are balancing and manipulating your tiles is that, in one respect, Scrabble has a lot in common with card games like bridge, pinochle, gin rummy, spades, and stud poker. You must keep track of the cards (in this case, tiles) that have already been played. It makes about as much sense for a Scrabble player to chase the word *exhaust* when both *H* tiles and both blanks have gone as it does for a card player to go for four kings when two of them are already exposed. It is too much to expect for players to keep a mental note on every tile played in a game, but everybody can, and should, keep perpetual track of the major tiles.

To start with, you should know how many tiles of each letter are in the game. It doesn't take long to commit to memory the fact that there is only one Z and one *Q*, one *J* and one *X*. And after a few games, everybody knows there are four tiles with an S on them and two blanks. But you should also be aware that there are 12 *E* tiles and nine *A* tiles and nine *I* tiles.

The full list, which is reproduced at the bottom left of the Scrabble board, is as follows:

A–9	J–1	S–4
B–2	K–1	T–6
C–2	L–4	U–4
D–4	M–2	V–2
E–12	N–6	W–2
F–4	O–8	X–1
G–3	P–2	Y–1
H–2	Q–1	Z–1
I–9	R–6	blank–2

Knowing when all tiles of a certain letter have been used can drastically alter a player's technique. For example, once the big guns have gone (the *Z*, *Q*, *J*, *X*), a player may gamble and risk exposing a triple-word score to his opponent providing his own score for that turn is a healthy one. The rationale is that with all the big ones out, and especially if most of the *H*'s, *F*'s, *W*'s, and the *K* are also on the board, the opponent cannot unleash a very damaging score even if he does seize the triple-word square on the next play.

By the same evaluation, a player with a late-in-the-game *S* feels much more secure about certain bold moves if he sees the other three *S* tiles on the board and if both blanks have also been neutralized. There is no way his competitor can pluralize most words for the remainder of the game, and, in addition, the opponent's chances for an eleventh hour bingo are also greatly diminished.

□

There is one letter that every Scrabble player, from his early Scrabble days, gets into the habit of tracking with the tenacity of a bird dog. That is the letter *U*. Each *U* is worth only one point, and there are only four of them, but they often prove to be the bane of many a Scrabble player's life. The reason is obvious: without one, you are stranded if you draw the *Q* tile from the bag.

This quirk of the English language can cause ulcers, hair-pulling, nail-biting, and teeth-gnashing and sometimes can make you wish you could just *QIT* (without a *U*). On occasions you seem to get all four *U*'s in a game, but don't get a whiff of the *Q*—or you draw the *Q* early and then remain bereft of *U* tiles or blanks for the whole game.

Sometimes I feel that Butts or Brunot should have given the *Q* a higher face value than its current 10 points. Perhaps 15 or 20 to compensate for the risks you run by holding on to it. After all, if you draw a Q as your first letter in the game, you know you only have six chances (four U's and two blanks) of drawing a letter that can mate with it out of the remaining 99 tiles, and those odds aren't exactly enticing. In addition, as long as you hold on to the Q, awaiting the arrival of a U, you are virtually playing with a six-letter rack and are thwarted from even attempting a bingo.

Because of this, a lot of good players who draw the Q early in the game will pass it back into the bag and forfeit a turn rather than carry its burden through future turns. This tactic especially makes sense if you can't get much of a score from your other tiles. It is also generally smart to pass the Q back in to the bag in the middle of the game or the final third of the game if you draw it and two or more U's are already on the board. The imperative time to ditch it, even though you forfeit a turn and even if the game is close, is in a maneuver that I call the "polecat pass." That is when all U's and the blanks are out or when there is the bare minimum of seven tiles remaining in the bag and you don't have a blank or a U to match up with the Q. Your chances of being trapped with the Q at the end of the game (and thereby being penalized 20 points if your opponent goes out) are at this time somewhat substantial.

The other question is when do you play away a U in your hand and when do you hold it as insurance in case you draw the Q. I'll admit that I tend to hold a U back even though it leads to weak vowel combinations in the rack like *iu* and *au*. (The best vowel combinations, incidentally, are *ea*, *ai*, and *ie*). Sometimes—and I know this sounds unrealistic and lacking in logic—it depends on the "feel" of the game. It's almost like in poker when you play a hunch and go for a straight rather than work on a safer hand.

Understandably, you are going to play a U if it is going to give you a massive score without waiting for the Q. Early in the game the risk of playing away a U is not that great because there is a fifty-fifty chance you won't draw the Q tile anyway. But for the final two-thirds of the game it *is* smart to hold on to a U until the Q has surfaced. A bonus from this is that if your opponent plays the Q you have a U of your own to build on his high-score letter.

If at any time you do play a U before the Q is out, make sure you play it in such a way that your opponent can't utilize it if he happens to be stranded with the Q in his hand. Play it up against the board walls or tucked in near other inhospitable letters, where it is safe and unplayable. Late in the game you can often tell whether or not your opponent has the letter Q by watching the expression on his face as you tuck a rare U in an unplayable lie.

This brings up another major point in rack management. Don't give yourself away by bad rack habits such as always putting the Q or the Z at the left-hand end of your rack or always keeping vowels at one end of the rack and consonants at the other. It's like playing pinochle or spades: you are a dead giveaway if you always keep your hearts at one end of your hand and spades at the other. I have seen a lot of players who might as well put their letters up in neon lights, judging by the way they flaunt the tiles on their racks. For example, don't automatically separate the tiles into words on your rack. If you have a five-letter word and two extra tiles, don't shunt the two letters to one end and leave the rack looking like 00 00000. It is much better to keep the seven tiles evenly spaced like so, 0 0 0 0 0 0 0, or break a seven-letter word like *tension* to look like *ten sion*. That is also a good safeguard if your opponent happens to get a glimpse of your letters. I have seen people who immediately send the *Q* to purgatory at the left end of the rack. The lineup looks like 0 000000, and an astute opponent can quickly guess what is going on. Sometimes, of course, it is a good idea to deliberately set up a phony rack like that just to confuse him.

The appearance of your rack is especially important near the end of the game when you are down to your last seven tiles. If you think you can go out in three turns, don't break your rack up into a formation of 00 00 000. Break the tiles up in your mind, but keep them in an evenly spaced wall like 0 0 0 0 0 0 0. Of course, if the game is in its death throes and your letters are *Q, Z, X, J, K, W, H*, there's no harm in letting your opponent think you've got three smashing words in your rack. If that's the case, then by all means break them up into ostentatious groupings, such as *QZ XJKW H*.

And don't underestimate such psychological ploys. The following is more "board management" than "rack management," but as an experiment try the meaningful stare stunt. It goes like this. There's a great opening for a zinger of a word on the bottom left corner of the board. You have a word organized in your rack, but it is your opponent's turn. What you do is shuffle your tiles feverishly and keep looking intently at the board—not at the bottom left corner, but at the top right. Your opponent is bound to note your agitation, and sometimes it will lure his attention to the area of the board that appears to have you captivated.

An extension of this is to look at a region of the board, as far removed as possible from where you hope to go next turn, and to make some remark like, "That word *zloty* you played a couple of turns ago was a terrific move. How many points was it worth again?" Or you say, "When did you play that word *nester*? I'd have either challenged it or put an S on it if I'd seen it." Both *zloty* and nester, of course, are pinned to a corner of the board far away from the area you hope to raid on your next turn, and a casual comment like that can sometimes just be enough to coach your opponent to a harmless area of the grid.

14 THE FINISHING POST

The final moves and maneuvers in a Scrabble game are something that I relish—even when I am losing.

If you play cannily in the dying stages of a game, you'll be surprised how many times you can come from behind and steal a one- or two-point victory. And one of the most thrilling wins is when you can go out and catch your opponent with a handful of high-value tiles, and your bonus of double his residue of unplayed letters is just enough to beat him by a couple of points. I love it.

Inventor Butts and his wife, Nina, must have had some quiet, unexciting finishes to their games. They play a version in which no differentiation is made between the player who goes out and the one who is trapped with unplayed tiles. It makes no difference who finishes first . . . play continues until all the tiles have gone or until neither player can make a move. In other words, you may go out and seemingly catch your opponent with a bundle, but then he can leisurely pick away at the board in multiple turns until his tiles are exhausted.

Butts explained, "We just keep playing until you can't play any more, and that's the end of it. This idea of counting the letters left when somebody goes out and you get double the score of the other players is absolutely silly to me. It's childish. It doesn't make any difference to the scores. You get two or three or four or five more points. I don't think I've ever seen a game where it made any difference."

That's not the case in my house. You catch somebody with a *J* in his hand, and it's worth 16 points to you, and that's not a bad score for a move in the final stages of a game. This is why end-of-game strategy is extremely important.

□

As the tiles dwindle in the bag, you must, more than ever, look ahead to future moves to ensure that you won't be caught with unplayable letters in the final turns. Rack-balancing rules still apply, but you have to improvise. Letters that were great defensive weapons early in the game, letters like the *C* and the *V*, are now liabilities. Their previous strengths, the fact that they cannot be used in two-letter words, now become their weaknesses, and you should try to play them away before you are down to your final seven letters.

Also, it is disaster to be caught in the final showdown with all vowels or all consonants. Actually, I believe it is worse in a close game to go into the final stretch with a hand heavy on vowels. That means you have all single-value tiles, and it becomes increasingly difficult to get any sort of competitive score in the final turns. A player with a hand weighted with consonants admittedly has trouble trying to go out, but he has the advantage of being able to drop an *H* or a *W* for healthy, last-minute scores. Also, if you have seven vowels, it can take four or five turns to unload them all.

The thing to do is to shuffle and reshuffle your tiles and try to retain in your head as many word combinations as possible. Bingos are usually impossible at this stage, and often the board is so tight that only two- and three-letter word openings are available.

It is also inevitable at this stage in the game that your opponent is hunting as desperately as you are for openings; so it is not sufficient to spot one place where you can go and then blithely wait for your next turn to claim it. The odds are overwhelming that your opponent will grab it. If you have a word, keep poring over the board to see if you can find two or three or four places where it can be lodged or where another letter combination can be placed.

The most important thing is to think ahead.

If you have the letters *C*,*A*,*P* in your hand and you also have a *U*, don't play the word *cap*—play the word *cup* because it will be easier later to place a solo *A* than a *U*. One time, though, when you don't do that is when all the tiles have gone and the *Q* is still absent. The odds are good you can trap your opponent with the *Q*, prevent him from going out, and collect the 20-point penalty. Under those circumstances, you play your *U* where it can't be used. Or you hold on to it.

If another *U* cannot be accounted for, then it means your opponent is still holding the *Q* and a *U*. That usually means he has a dearth of vowels in his hand and can't get a word down. Don't oblige him by opening up a chance where he can build on your vowels and get rid of his *Q* and his *U*. If you can, keep blocking the game up and picking away until all your seven tiles have gone.

You can see that keeping track of what letters have gone becomes critical in the final stages. Some good players know exactly what their opponents are holding by keeping a mental ledger of what tiles are still out. For example, if the *K* has not been played, you haven't got it, and all tiles have been drawn, don't play a word like *in* if it can easily be extended to *ink* or *kin*. If the *J* is still missing, don't expose an *O* or an *A*, which your opponent can extend to *jo* or *ja*—and be especially careful that you don't expose those letters below a triple-letter square where the *J* alone is worth 24 points.

You just have to know at this stage if all the big letters have gone as well as the four *S* tiles and the blanks. If a blank or an *S* is still unaccounted for, then look around the board, and see if you have any high-scoring words still available for pluralization.

If the word *question*, for example, is on the board and you haven't got an *S* or a blank to use to pluralize it yourself, try to play a two-letter word off the exposed *N* so that it blocks the plural square even though it doesn't cover it. That sort of tactic, though, is for a defensive finish if you can't do anything scintillating yourself. The best finish is a strong burst where you catch your opponent with a rackful of tiles.

Ironically, there are times, when you are trailing, when it does not pay to go out. If all the big tiles are gone and you estimate your opponent has about 10 points left in his hand, it doesn't make much sense to go out if you are trailing by 50 points. In times like those, having apparently lost the game anyway, I have often hung in there on the assumption that where there's life, there's hope. By hanging on and studying the board, you sometimes spot something, a gem that has been hidden there.

Or, as happened to me once, my opponent played the innocuous late-stage word *la*, which was close enough to a previously played *jug* for me to put a troublesome *U* in the middle and an *R* at the end to make the word *jugular*, which hit a double-word score. Suddenly I had 30 points to make it a horse race again.

That's what is great about this game. You can be trailing by 100 points and then maybe you get a couple of breaks . . . you draw the *X* and play it well . . . you win a challenge . . . your opponent passes . . . and his lead dissipates faster than a cup of hot water on the desert sand.

□

One of the dictionary definitions for the word *Scrabble is* "to scrape together," and that's sometimes what you have to do to scrabble up a winning margin.

15. HOW AND WHEN TO CHALLENGE

TRUE DISPUTANTS ARE LIKE SPORTSMEN, THEIR
WHOLE DELIGHT IS IN THE PURSUIT.
                    —*Alexander Pope, 1688–1744*

Knowing when to challenge your opponent's use of words in Scrabble is a bit like knowing when somebody at your poker table is bluffing. Part of it is knowledge of the game, part is intuition, and part is pure *chutzpah*.

The rules that deal with the sometimes embarrassing situation of accusing your opponent of cheating—or at least of being a prevaricator —are clear-cut. The standard Scrabble rules flatly state that any word formed on the board may be challenged before the start of the next player's turn.

The official rules for Scrabble tournaments used to be a little more restrictive. They permitted a challenge of only one word played, or modified, in the previous turn, which meant that a shrewd player could drop an interlocking combination of letters that produced more than one disputed word, and it would be up to the challenger to decide which word was the most disputable. Tournament Scrabble rules now state—and I believe this is a sound rule—that any word, formed or transformed in a single turn, is open to challenge.

Under tournament rules if a challenged word is ruled unacceptable, then the player responsible takes back the offending letters and misses his turn. If the challenged word is acceptable, according to whatever dictionary is being regarded as law, then the score for the hand stands, and the challenger misses a turn.

Under the standard rules, the ones that are printed in the lids of most Scrabble sets and are followed in many homes, the rules covering disputed words are less severe on challengers. The rules state that if a challenged word is rejected, then the guilty player takes back his tiles and loses his turn. There is *no* penalty to the challenger if the word is indeed in the dictionary. In other words, a player could challenge every single move by his opponent and keep him honest without ever risking any personal sacrifice.

At the other end of the scale is the variation of the challenge rule, which demands that whenever a player challenges a word, and loses, then he not only misses a turn, but his score is reduced by the amount that his opponent is legally entitled to for the play. That means that if the disputed word is worth 50 points, the instigator not only gets his 50 points, but his challenger loses 50 to make the play—in effect, a 100-point word. In my view, this is too punitive because it scares players away from challenges, even on preposterous words. You will also find, in a three- or four-handed game, that one player will sit back, let his opponents keep each other honest and bleed themselves to death, while he accepts everything without qualm and plays a parasitic winner's game.

There definitely are times when you should, as a cold-blooded tactic, permit an opponent's phony word to stand unchallenged even though its presence may be aesthetically repugnant. For example, if your opponent puts down a nonword or a wrongly spelled word for which he gets 15 points and which as a result opens up a chance for you to drop a seven-letter boardbuster worth 35 points plus a 50-point bonus, then for God's sake don't challenge. Block your mind to pure English and proper spelling, and take the 85 points and run.

In a recent game my opponent hurriedly played the word *squirm* and, in her eagerness and playing with an upside-down board, spelled it without the letter *U*. It was late in the game, a close game that had been excruciatingly tight. Before challenging, I looked around and realized I could attach a seven-letter bingo to that phony *sqirm*, which would hit a triple-word square and clinch the game. I let the spelling boo-boo pass, took the 50-point bonus for a bingo, won the game, and learned a lesson: Control all knee-jerk reactions to an opponent's spelling errors. You may be able to turn them to your own advantage.

□

Frank Kuehnrich, the New York City 1975 champion, is a defensive Scrabble player who confesses to being a "heavy challenger." After he won the title, Kuehnrich admitted to me, "I challenge more than the average player ... but it all depends. If I'm playing somebody with a big vocabulary, I won't challenge so much."

Kuehnrich warned against a particularly dangerous form of Scrabble player—the challenge fisherman. "There are some players who are not so good, but they have a lot of words in their vocabularly, especially unusual words," he said. "They'll try to tempt you into a challenge that you'll lose, and then they will get an extra turn." Such players will memorize words like *rabbet*. You challenge them, thinking they have made a spelling slip, only to discover they are one hop ahead of you. Your misspelled *rabbit* is a carpenter's term to describe a grooved piece of wood.

Another thing to remember if you are challenging is which dictionary is being used as the guideline. Scrabble tournament experts boast about the 69 two-letter words that are permissible in Funk & Wagnalls. They can dazzle you by spouting *aa, nu, mu, ex, ut, xi, wo, ka*. This tactic—and I have been guilty of it myself—can intimidate an opponent. Once the other player is convinced that you are an expert on two-letter words, then it doesn't take much to slip a phony past him. For months, playing against my wife, I used the word *ra*. It is in the dictionary, but it is capitalized and therefore illegal. And once somebody has lost a challenge on the word *ad*, which is legal, it's not hard to twist his arm to get him to acquiesce on a word like *ed*, which is illegal.

One time you should always challenge is at the end of the game if your opponent is going out and if his word is even vaguely suspect. If you don't challenge, then the game is over anyway, so the last-ditch attempt to stop him costs you nothing. An opponent of mine went out in a game by playing the word *mont*. The game was close, and this was a desperate effort to get double the letter value of my remaining tiles and win the game. I had no idea whether or not *mont* was a word, but if I didn't challenge, the game was over. As it happened, there was no such word, the tiles were picked up, and the turn forfeited. I went out next turn and collected double the face values of the disputed *M,O,N,* and *T*.

To muddy the waters further and make challenges more dangerous, different dictionaries have different standards. In Funk & Wagnalls, *ja*, the German for "yes," is listed; it is not permitted in the unabridged Random House dictionary. On the other hand, the word *te* is not one of the 69 two-letter words permitted in Funk & Wagnalls, but it is acceptable in Random House. What it boils down to is knowing the deck of cards you are playing with, knowing your opponent's bluffing record, and knowing when to roll out an old-fashioned, across-the-table, "call me if you dare" staredown.

And I challenge you to find a more exciting "put your money where your mouth is" confrontation than that.

16 HOW AND WHEN TO PASS

Despite Mr. Butts's good fortune, one of the most important things to learn about Scrabble is to know when to pass—when to forfeit the chance to add something, anything, to your score and instead toss in some of your tiles in the hope of drawing a better selection.

The practice of passing is a strategem that has grown since the advent of Tournament Scrabble and the growing importance of the 50-point bonus seven-letter words.

Before knowing when you should pass, you should know when you *may* pass. Under basic Scrabble rules, any player may use his turn to replace any of the seven letters in his rack. He does this by discarding the unwanted tiles face down on the table, draws an equal number of fresh tiles, mixes the discards with the remaining tiles in the pool, and awaits his next turn.

In those original rules, no provision was made for the player with a lucrative, but unplayable, seven-letter word combination in his hand, who is prepared to miss a turn in the hope that the board will open up for his next turn. The newer tournament rules permit such passing without any exchange of tiles, but if both players pass three consecutive turns each, the game is terminated. House rules should determine whether that means the game is scored as a draw, as in a chess stalemate, or whether the game should go to the person with the leading score.

The only restriction to passing is the stipulation that there must still be at least seven tiles left in the tile bag. Once there are seven, or fewer, tiles in the pool, no passing of any kind is permitted. This restriction (not envisaged in the original rules) is necessary to thwart a player, caught with something like the Q late in the game, who tries to pass it back in when there is only one other tile in the bag. Without the seven-tile restriction, he could ditch it and keep passing until his opponent had drawn it.

□

If a player elects to swap any or all of the tiles in his hand for a fresh supply from the bag, then that constitutes a complete turn. He is not permitted to place any tiles on the board or score in the same turn. Another variation permits any player caught with three or more of the same letter in his hand to discard the extra letters (in excess of two) and redraw without losing a turn. The exchange must be made immediately after the tiles are drawn.

So that's when you *can* pass; now when *should* you?

There's one cardinal rule: never pass unless you have to, and when you have to do it, then do it speedily and unflinchingly.

I always regard a pass as a 50-point penalty that sometimes has to be taken to shore up a crumbling position. The 50 points, in my mind, are made up by the 25-point score you could expect to get for a moderate play, and didn't, added to the minimum of 25 points you can expect your opponent to get during his bonus turn when you forfeit yours. Despite that, when I feel I have to revitalize my hand, I'll do it, and often the decision to pass can turn a game around in your favor.

□

The prime time to pass is when your hand is filled with duplicates, especially when it looks something like *U,U,I,I,N,M,L*. Obviously, you are not totally stumped with that hand, and you could play away some of the letters, but your score will probably be low and your rack still polluted.

I discussed earlier in this strategy section the importance of what Scrabble experts call "rack balancing." Sometimes, though, the bad luck of the draw and the game's development make it impossible to keep an equal number of vowels and consonants on hand. You are left with a set of tiles so unbalanced that the vowels are about to tip it over.

This is the time for drastic surgery. It's time to pass. There are special cases, but it is generally best to pass in all seven tiles when you are doing the spring-cleaning. Some people, though, play hunches and keep back a favorite letter or, if it's early in the game and you have both the *Q* and a *U*, you might want to keep both of them. With that pair, though, you should be able to play yourself out of trouble without passing.

To me it's a bit like five-card draw poker. Usually, if I have a good pair, I'll keep them and discard the other three cards for a redraw. But sometimes, if one of the other cards is a high one or if some inner voice speaks to me, I'll keep back a third "swing" card. In Scrabble there are only two tiles that you absolutely must keep back when discarding on a pass. They are the S and the blank. These are the most versatile and, therefore, most valuable letters in the game and should never be discarded. It can be a dangerous game, but I will also sometimes keep back letter combinations like *ing* and *ion* because of the lure of bingos with those letters.

□

The really dangerous game when passing, despite what I have just said, is fishing. That is when you have six great letters for a possible bingo and one tile that makes the fly in the proverbial ointment look good. The temptation is great to pass, throw back the offending letter, and "fish" for a better one.

The temptation may be great, but the danger is even greater. Ask a poker player about the chances of trying to fill an "inside straight" in poker. If you make it, you are a star, but if you miss, you have nothing. And, in fact, in both Scrabble and poker, you are far worse off than if you had gone for something less adventurous.

The risks of fishing are obviously affected by what you have in your hand—by what size hook you are using. Also, the decision on whether or not to fish is affected by whether or not you are winning and by how much.

I was trailing badly in a game and decided to go fishing because I urgently needed a bingo to give my score a transfusion. There were six great letters in my rack and one troublemaker, the *J*. The "bait" letters were a blank and the tiles *O,T,I,O,N*. That lessened the risks while fishing. By treating the blank as an S, all I needed—to make a seven-letter word—was a *P* or an *M* or an *L* to make *potions, motions,* or *lotions.* Reshuffling brought other possibilities—like using the blank as an *R* if I drew a *T* to make *tortion* or as a *T* if I drew an *R*. As it happened, I drew an *E* and used the blank as an *M* to make the word *emotion.* This was a case of fishing with an exceedly large hook.

Another time to fish for a single letter is when your remaining six letters make up one of those key words that will go with virtually any other letter of the alphabet to make a seven-letter word. Two of these, mentioned earlier, are *satire* and *retina. Santer* is a third, and New York champ Kuehnrich claims to have a few secret ones of his own.

If you have the word *satire* in your hand, then you should know that 18 of the 26 letters in the alphabet can be added to some combination or other of those six letters and produce a bingo word.

All told, according to Funk & Wagnalls there are more than 50 bingo words possible if you start with *satire* as your six-letter base, and they are listed in the vocabulary part. With the word *retina*, at least 45 bingo words are possible when those six-letters are mated in some order with 16 other letters of the alphabet. Obviously, if you can memorize all, or some, of those words then fishing becomes a less dangerous sport. Even so, passing remains a serious tactic.

□

There is one late-in-the-game situation when it is imperative that you pass—providing you follow the rules and there are still seven tiles remaining in the tile bag. This is the bailout move that I call the "polecat pass" because that's about as popular as it makes you.

Once again, it concerns the troublesome letter Q. If, near the game's end, you draw the Q and all the U's and both blanks have gone, you should treat it like a pariah. You must pass it back in. There is a chance you may draw it again, but it is a chance you have to take. As it stands, if you keep the Q, it is impossible for you to go out, and that makes your Q worth 20 points to your opponent if he goes out. At best, it will cost you a penalty of 10 points deducted from your total for being caught with it.

Sometimes you will find, when a hopeless-looking hand makes a pass seem inevitable, that you can salvage the turn by a low-scoring play called "dumping." By using this alternative method to revamp you hand—a strategy described in the chapter on rack management—you can unload several duplicated low-value tiles, pick up a few points, and avoid the stigma of having to forfeit a turn. There are good "dumping words," and some are listed in the vocabulary section.

None of this, though, is as important as this simple rule about passing. When you feel you have to do it, then do it. Quickly. It's amazing the number of times you'll hear somebody cursing their luck and their poor tiles, and a bit later in the game they'll say, "If only I'd passed way back when. ... "

The passing ploy in Scrabble is a bit like a visit to the dentist. Nobody can kid you that it's not going to hurt. But the longer you delay it, the more it will hurt—and not until the trouble is fixed can you smile again.

Part IV

SCRABBLING ABOUT

17 THE SNEAKY, SNIDE, SURREPTITIOUS, SWINDLING SCRABBLE CHEAT

ANYTHING WORTH HAVING IS WORTH CHEATING FOR.
                                                —W. C. Fields

It may come as a shock to gentlemen players like Jim Brunot and Alfred Butts, but, like most games, Scrabble is not immune to the cheat. It's a sad fact of life that in any game where one person wins and one loses you are eventually going to run up against somebody trying to beat the odds, stack the deck, load the dice, get an edge, or inflate his score by cheating.

In Scrabble the cheat can be the white-haired grandmother, who supposedly can't see without her glasses, peeking into the tile bag while drawing her letters, or the sharpie sneaking an upside-down tile on to the board and pretending it's a blank. Or it can be the student who never has trouble with the New Math, but somehow always seems to botch the job when it comes to Scrabble scoring. . . .

Hopefully, you won't be confronted by a cheat across your Scrabble table. If you are and if it is someone you cherish, then maybe it's best to shrug the whole thing off as an eccentricity or an oversight. The least you can do is give him or her the space to pass it off as an "honest mistake." However, if you are being ripped off by a board bandit, then at least you should be aware of some of the more insidious forms of Scrabble cheating.

Of course, if you haven't won a game in 20 years and have a larcenous bent, then I suppose you could regard this chapter as a service—a sort of do-it-yourself (illegally) Scrabble winner's kit.

□

The most common form of Scrabble cheating is the old "looking in the tile bag trick"—the one attributed earlier to the allegedly shortsighted grandmother. It's surprising how many people are guilty of this illegality, and you'd also be surprised how many people dismiss it as an "accident."

The game is going badly. The letters you grope for in the bag remain enticingly, infuriatingly out of reach. So you take a quick, almost accidental peep into the bag for a glimpse of your elusive desperately needed tile. When you spot it, your groping hand veers suddenly to that corner of the bag, and you lunge at the tile, with your hand behaving like one of those quaint, chain-operated cranes that grabbed for candy balls in the old, circus penny arcades. You can excuse such a lapse any way you like, but let's face it. That is cheating.

One way to prevent such tactics is to revert to the original Scrabble rules governing the selection of tiles to refill your rack. Right at the start the original rules state that the first thing you do is to turn all the tiles face down alongside the board and shuffle them. Thereafter, the supply of tiles remains face down on the table, with players selecting their new tiles in full view of their opponents.

This system of tile selection is still far from foolproof. In fact, it has several weaknesses that are easily exploitable by the average Scrabble cheat. The first weakness is the tiles themselves. Although they are expensive-looking, aesthetically pleasing polished wood tiles imported from Germany with a history of their own, the tiles *are* individually identifiable. Over the years millions of tiles have been rejected, first by Jim Brunot and later by Selchow & Righter, because of their blatant wood grain patterns. Even so, a canny Scrabble player can still distinguish subtle but definitely identifiable "tile prints" in the grains of the accepted tiles.

In fairness to the manufacturers, it should be pointed out that each new set sold contains a form that states, "If you find there are missing or defective tiles in this Scrabble Crossword game, please report them to us and we will adjust same." However, I have found that people only return blemished tiles if they are so disfigured that the tile designation is almost broadcast in neon lights.

☐

Scrabble Inventor Butts had an experience with the possibility of marked tiles back in the 1930s, when he was producing a Scrabble-forerunner called Lexiko. The game was a sophisticated version of Anagrams, using tiles, which Butts made with plywood, architect's blueprint paper, and a jigsaw. He sold them for $1.50 a set and one day received one back in the mail. The owner said he had bought the game from a friend and believed it was a sample. "I have a feeling these tiles are marked and therefore would give me an unfair advantage," he wrote. "Please send me a normal, unmarked set." The tiles were not marked but Butts sent a fresh set just to ease the Lexiko buff's conscience.

☐

One drawback to the idea of keeping the tile reservoir upside down alongside the board is the simple fact that the person who does the shuffling has a distinct advantage. Anybody with a reasonably retentive memory can remember approximately in what area he has seeded, say, the Z, Q, and X. He can then make flamboyant shuffling gestures, with his hands agitating the tiles, without ever losing track of where the high-scoring tiles are stored.

If you don't believe that, then watch an expert shuffle dominoes. Even a good, albeit dishonest, domino shuffler can stir up a storm and still know exactly where the crucial double-six is lying. Because of these drawbacks, I adhere to the idea of using a bag to store the tiles. You can buy plush velvet tile bags from the Scrabble manufacturer, but an equally good receptacle is one of those velvet bags from a well-aged bottle of Scotch whisky. The bag I use is a Hessian sack, which once held a bottle of Spanish sherry. It's a foot deep, and my wife sewed a drawstring ribbon into the neck. It is virtually cheat-proof because the only way you can see into it is to deliberately and fairly obviously peer down inside through a neck that is just wide enough to force a hand through.

□

Scrabble analysts claim that skill wins Scrabble games and that the luck of the draw constitutes only 12 percent of the victory margin. Nevertheless, some people will do anything to eliminate even that 12 percent, and that is why the second most common form of Scrabble cheating also involves tile selection. So be on the lookout for the "cupped hand caper," an illegal procedure where a player plunges his hand into the tile bag and hauls out a cupped handfull of tiles. He may be entitled to draw, say, three tiles. but by using his fingers as a shovel, he actually scoops six or seven tiles from the bag. The Scrabble cheat then quickly selects three tiles from the handfull and drops the rest in the bag. In that one speedy motion, an accomplished cheat can select three desirable tiles that have surfaced face up in his cupped hand or, in a reverse action, can avoid letter that would duplicate tiles already in his hand.

The proper procedure is for each player to count each tile in his fingers while his hand is still hidden in the tile bag. He must then place each selected new tile *face down* alongside his rack in full view of his opponent. Then he counts the number of new tiles to make sure he has drawn the correct number, and only then does he add them to his rack. If through a miscalculation, accidental or deliberate, a player winds up with more than seven tiles on his rack, he must immediately tell his opponent, who then blindly selects the excess tiles at random from the rack and returns them to the bag.

The overstocked hand is a tactic that all players should be alert for. A brazen cheat will deliberately overdraw letters when restocking his hand and then play with eight letters until he can make a seven-letter word to collect his 50-point bingo bonus. What does he do with the extra letter? He palms it and drops it back in the bag when drawing his new supply of tiles. Or he keeps it and only draws six fresh letters instead of seven. If you think that is farfetched, just think—when was the last time you counted the number of tiles in your opponent's rack? You just assumed he was playing with seven, right?

□

Another tactic of an adroit palmer is to exchange problem letters without forfeiting a turn by passing. This is done by surreptitiously hiding a problem letter in your hand after playing a normal turn. The unwanted letter is held in the palm and dropped back into the bag while the player is digging for new letters. A dishonest player who has laid out a three-letter word can palm an unwanted tile from his rack, drop it back in the bag, pick up four new letters (instead of the legal three), and usually escape detection.

Any player with the nerve and lack of scruples to pull that off would probably not be above attempting the "phony blank routine." This can be tried in any game, but it is more likely in a game where the rules of Ecology Scrabble are in effect, where the blank can be recycled to be used again and again in the same game.

It goes like this. The Scrabble cheat has the letters Z,E,A,L,K,T,S in his rack. If only the K were an O, he would have the word *zealots* with a minimum of 66 points without any double- or triple-letter or word bonuses.

He turns the K upside down to create an instant blank (providing both blanks aren't already on the board) and lays down his seven-letter bingo as *zeal-blank-ts*. He gambles that soon he'll collect a real O from the tile bag and can then replace the phony letter, undetected, pick up the K, invert it, and play it as a K later.

The major risk is that both blanks will appear before he has a chance to retrieve the spurious letter (or, in Ecology Scrabble that his opponent will drop an O and claim the "blank"). Actually, the latter risk is not that great: an oblivious opponent could play with his upside-down K as a blank and never know it. If he did discover it, he could think of it as his own mistake. The simple way to thwart this bit of larceny is to turn over every blank every time it is played.

In Tournament Scrabble it is the opponent's responsibility to check the legitimacy of each "blank" tile as soon as it has been played. If a blank is a phony, the player who used it, either intentionally or unintentionally, must immediately withdraw it as well as all other tiles used in that move. The score for the turn is canceled, and the turn is forfeited, with the player recording "pass" on his score sheet.

If a phony blank goes undetected and is then discovered later in the game when the two authentic blanks turn up, the imposter must be left on the board as an extra blank. There is no retroactive penalty for the player who originally played it.

□

In Monopoly the banker has more chances to cheat and more temptation to cheat because he's the player who gets to handle the money. In Scrabble the same thing applies to the player who acts as scorekeeper. It's easy for him, especially if not playing against an eagle-eyed opponent, to trim a couple of points here and there from the competitor's tally. And by the same token he can occasionally pad his own score. Similarly, other players can steal a few bonus points by calling a double-letter as a triple or just by counting fast and with seeming authority while inflating the score for a turn.

The best way to overcome these temptations is for both players to keep scoreboards alongside them and for each to add up his own and his opponent's scores. Besides keeping everybody honest, this is a good idea because psychologically it can give you a lift if every turn you can see the margin between you close (if you are fighting back from a losing streak) or widen (if you are pulling away). Both players should also count the board score for each individual turn.

□

There is one board tactic that some people call cheating and others regard as mere messy play. That is the tactic whereby a player drops a word on the board and then, after it is down, starts rearranging the letters. This is a no-no.

The next chapter, on board etiquette, spells out the rules on when a turn is legally finished. I mention it here, though, because the real Scrabble cheat will often use such a ploy to get an edge on his opponent.

Often by watching an opponent's face while dropping a dubious word, a good cheat can gauge whether he is likely to be challenged or not. If the opponent has a real "gotcha" look in his eye, then the cheater can swiftly rearrange his letters, on the board, to salvage a lower-scoring, but legal word.

□

And while we are on the subject of challenging and cheating, watch out for the dictionary browser—the person who under the guise of looking up a disputed word takes about 15 minutes to find it in the dictionary. He's the person who volunteers to look up a challenged word beginning with a *W* and starts looking for it under *J*. Next thing you know, he drops the word *jereeds* on the board for a triple-word score of 45 plus a bonus of 50 and says, "Oh, a *jereed* is a blunt, wooden javelin used in games by horsemen in certain Muslim countries in the Middle East. Everybody knows that." Especially if they have just spotted it in the dictionary.

□

By devoting so much space to dishonest Scrabble tactics, I hate to give the impression that the world is filled with tile tricksters and board bandits. Still, these things are worth knowing, so that if you do get beaten, at least you know you were beaten honestly.

18 BOARD ETIQUETTE

In tennis it is considered bad manners to cross behind a court while a player is serving. In golf you never walk between an opponent's ball and the hole when on the green. And in poker it is correct for the dealer always to pass the shuffled cards back to his left for the previous dealer to cut them. This is part of the ritual and etiquette that surrounds every sport or game, including Scrabble. Some of the following no-no's are purely acts of courtesy, but others are rules, and violations of them can lose games.

□

It should go without saying that when an opponent is using his allotted time to make his turn, you do not whistle; sing; drum your fingers on the table; distract him with comments about Aunt Bess, politics, or religion; or snatch the board away from him and turn it around so that it faces you.

The biggest etiquette problem arises when people get impatient for an opponent to make his play so that they can get on with theirs. This often disputed situation can be eradicated quite simply: before you start a game, set a time limit per turn. If you follow tournament rules, each player has three minutes in which to make a move, and he has to move within that time or forfeit his turn. If you find that time limits are too restrictive—even limits of five, ten, or fifteen minutes per turn—then don't complain when your opponent takes half an hour for a difficult move.

The irony is that when you are trying to smoke an elusive bingo from your hand, it seems like seconds. When your opponent is trying to do the same thing, it seems like hours. The big thing in favor of time clocks is that they are great argument stoppers. They also keep the game moving.

□

I remember when I was about ten years old playing Scrabble one winter with a favorite aunt and uncle in a town called Christchurch, New Zealand. Play stalled while my Aunt Edna took an interminable time to make a move. Transfixed, the three of us stared at the board. Occasionally, one of us would get up, stretch, and toss another log on the fire. Back then I didn't have the temerity to demand that an elder "pull finger" and get on with the game. Finally, after about half an hour—it seemed longer—she turned to my Uncle Ken and said, "If you really can't go, dear, I think it's only fair that you pass."

Her perplexed and slightly frazzled husband replied, "Me? It's your jolly turn." It was too.

□

Some of the breaches of etiquette are really rule infractions, and things like drawing too many letters and peeking in the tile bag have been dealt with in the chapter on the Scrabble cheat. There are other board habits, though, that cause table feuds and antipathy, which I hope to eliminate or at least curtail by discussion here.

Take, for example, the "board cruiser," the player who can't make a decision on a word while the tiles are in his rack and who must try out his combinations on the board. He plays his letters, but before totaling up and accepting the score for the word, he moves the tiles to about three different locations on the board in quest of a better deal.

We follow a house rule that once a word is placed on the board, it must stay there unless removed under challenge. If a player puts down a word that is wrongly spelled, then that is his mistake, and he must pay for it if the mistake is spotted by his opponent.

This is one thing you should be extremely careful about at all times—especially when you have not bothered to turn the board around and are playing a word upside down. You'd be surprised the number of times somebody puts down something like the word *rouge* and spells it *ruoge*. In these instances, the wrongly spelled word should stay, and the player must accept the consequences if challenged.

Similar in style is "last minute Louie." He's the player who lays down a word, adds up the score, and just before it is recorded, shouts, "Hold it," and scoops up his tiles to put them somewhere else.

To eradicate the Louies of the Scrabble set, we have copied a long-standing rule in chess. That is the touch test. Once your fingers have left the tiles, your turn is complete. You cannot go back to rearrange the tiles.

This may sound harsh, but there is good reason for it. Sometimes a player may genuinely make a mistake and go to correct it, but other times "last minute Louie" will play a word and not holler until he sees an opponent start to lunge at another rewarding spot on the board. To stop that and to eliminate any suspicion of such feinting, we follow the finger-on-the-tile creed.

Another house rule worth considering involves faulty planning. Quite often a player, made careless by the taste of an upcoming bingo, will lay down a seven-letter word with a flourish, only to discover that there is room for only six of his tiles. In some gentlemanly games he is permitted to take back the ill-fitting word and try again.

In the Hinch household, any player making that mistake, having a foot too big for the shoe, must still play in that position on the board by trying to salvage a shorter word that fits. Here's an example. Say, in the flush of triumph, you start to lay down the bingo word *emotion*. You get as far as E–M–O–T–I–O– and run out of squares. To salvage something from that blooper that leaves you feeling sheepish, you are permitted to hastily rearrange tiles on that same row of squares. If lucky, you may get away with a six-letter word like *motion*, or you may have to settle for *emit* or *moot* or some such minor score.

The option is also there—and it is one I would take—to withdraw all tiles for the turn and forfeit. In that sort of pass, in which your tiles have been briefly on the board, you are not permitted to use the turn to exchange letters in the tile bag.

This rule makes players doubly careful when planning moves.

□

There is a whole ritual surrounding the drawing of tiles from the bag and for good reason. Tiles are the tools of Scrabble in the same manner that dice are the tools of craps and cards the tools of poker. Nobody is permitted to take the dice out of sight of other players at a craps table, and in poker nobody is permitted to rummage through the discards or the unplayed deck in the middle of a hand.

The same thing applies to Scrabble. The only time you look in the tile bag is before the game, when you are checking to make sure there are exactly 100 tiles in there. When a player is replenishing his rack, he must do so in full view of his opponent or opponents.

I've described in the cheating part some of the antics that Scrabble sharpies perform around the tile bag, but I've saved "overdraw Oscar" for this chapter because 80 percent of the time what he does is out of carelessness and not out of dishonesty. "Overdraw Oscar" is the fellow who three or four times a game suddenly announces, loudly and supposedly sincerely, that, shucks, he has made a mistake and has eight, nine, or ten tiles in his rack.

Sometimes, and this is still giving Oscar the benefit of the doubt, he will apologize and quickly drop the extra tiles back into the bag. By doing that, though, he has been able, no matter how innocently, to select the best seven tiles from the eight, nine, or ten that were in his rack.

The other solution is for the transgressor to hold up his rack and have the opponent draw the extra tiles off and return them to the bag. That way, however, the chronic overdraw artist has been able illegally to get a look at tiles still to be drawn.

Some people play under house rules whereby a player who overdraws is penalized, say 10 or 20 points, for each tile drawn in excess of his entitlement. Another variation is that when a player has an overstocked rack, he must pass back all letters into the bag and redraw a fresh seven tiles. In practice this unofficial rule can sometimes work in favor of the player who made the original goof. If he has poor letters, he can intentionally overdraw and then get a fresh set of tiles without forfeiting a turn. He also gets a look at another 7 percent of the tiles in the kitty.

□

Scoring is another segment of the game where etiquette, and obviously honesty, are important. We've dealt with the honesty of it. Now let's deal with the etiquette.

Sometimes an honest mistake can cause bad blood that can ruin a game, and a person who is slow at arithmetic can be at a disadvantage. Ideally, each player should keep a score pad alongside his rack and keep a turn-by-turn total of his own score and that of his opponent. As I said before, that not only keeps people honest, but it can help your game psychologically.

After you have played your word, you should call the score out loud as you add it up. If, for example, you play the word *manners* across the board, you should score it aloud and cumulatively as follows: *M* is 3, plus 1 is 4, plus 1 is 5, plus 1 is 6; the *E* is a triple-letter for 3, equals 9; plus 1 is 10, plus 1 is 11. *M* is on a double-word—22. Plus 50 for the bingo. Total, 72."

It also pays to recheck it. Remember that if you add a score incorrectly and give yourself too many points, your opponent is bound to correct you, but there are a hundred people who'll do that for every one who'll tell you that you have given yourself too few. Once the word has been accepted and tallied and the score entered on the sheet, it is too late for a belated challenge from an opponent.

□

I have saved for last one of the most common and most frustrating breaches of board etiquette: the habit of constantly tidying the board, especially when it is somebody else's turn.

Everybody likes a neat board, with the letters carefully and symmetrically aligned in their proper positions, but some board tidiers make Hazel, the maid, look downright slovenly. Throughout the game they incessantly fuss over the board and fidget with the tiles.

Obviously, there are occasions when a previously played tile has slipped out of alignment and needs attention, but generally the board tidier is a nuisance and a distraction to his opponent. It may sound paranoiac, but it seems to me that the urge to spring-clean always strikes people when it is somebody else's turn. What they tend to forget is the fact that just because a player is not physically touching the board, it does not mean he is not using it. When it is his turn, he owns the board; it is his to visualize whatever letter combinations he wishes, and he should be able to do that without the distraction of an opponent jiggling the tiles. In Tournament Scrabble the problem is not as frequent because tournament players use deluxe boards with a raised grid pattern that prevents the tiles from shifting out of line.

The thing to remember most in this case—and in other areas of board etiquette—is "do unto others." If you play with the tiles, whistle, sing, squirm, drum fingers on the tabletop, crunch toast, crack nuts, crack knuckles, slurp coffee, ask questions, or tickle your opponent, keep in mind that he or she can do the same to you. And when you are a smidgen away from a zillion point play, each intrusion or imagined intrusion is magnified a million times.

19 VARIATIONS ON A THEME

NO PLEASURE ENDURES, UNSEASONED BY VARIETY.
—*Publilius Syrus, First Century* B.C.

In the 40 years since he invented Scrabble, Alfred Butts has played or heard about almost every conceivable variation in the game. Luckily, though, Butts is not one of those egomaniacs who believes what he has created is a masterpiece that cannot be tampered with. Butts, like his successor, Jim Brunot, loves bending the Scrabble rules to suit the playing conditions.

As Butts points out, if you played the game the way he originally conceived it, you would not get a 50-point bonus for dropping all seven tiles in a single word, the game would not end just because one player used up all his tiles, and the first person out would not receive the end-of-game windfall of double the total of his opponents' remaining tiles.

"There are some people who say you must play by the directions," he said, "but I don't believe that." And Jim Brunot has often said that you should make up your own house rules and play that way.

With that blessing from the game's maker, Scrabble players have come up with such exotic variations as Ecology Scrabble, Double Bag Scrabble, Anagram Scrabble, Stopwatch Scrabble, and even Scrabble-in-reverse: a diabolical game called Unscrabble.

The following, then, are some tried and tested variations on the game of Scrabble with which you might like to experiment. Before you start, you should remember two things: first, always spell out house rules clearly before a game, to prevent arguments, which can become heated during a match. And second, remember the plea of both Butts and Brunot: "Look, it's only a game."

Jacks to Open

The orthodox Scrabble start goes as follows: each player draws a tile from the bag and the one nearest to the beginning of the alphabet gets to go first. All he has to do is use two or more tiles and place one of them on the center star.

The problem with the standard start is that the lead-off player may decide to open with a word like *xi* or *qua* or some other short word and thereby launch a game so tight that it almost strangles before it gets off the ground.

To make the start more interesting and to let the early game "breathe," a lot of Scrabble players opt for a compulsory big-word start, which I call "Jacks to Open," as in Jackpot Poker. Under this variation, the player who draws the tile closest to *A* has the chance to start (and double his opening score), but only if he has a word of five letters or more. If he cannot make a five-letter word, then he must say, "Pass" and relinquish the starting pole to the next competitor. In four-handed Scrabble this goes on until one player can make a five-letter opener.

If nobody can form a five-letter word, then the prerogative passes back to the original opener, who then attempts to make a four-letter word, for which he will still get the double-word bonus—as would one of his opponents if he could have made a five-letter word. If Player No. 1 still cannot make a word four letters in length, he again passes, and so on, with the mandatory word length shrinking until somebody can go. If you cannot "open," you must pass, and you may not use that pass to exchange tiles.

Aces to Open

The start of "Aces to Open" is merely a more deadly version of "Jacks to Open" and involves upping the ante. The player who draws the starting letter closest to *A* can only go if he can make a seven-letter word. If that is not possible, the player must pass and give each opponent a chance for a seven-letter, bingo opener. Then, in rotation, each player has an opportunity for a six-letter word to open, then a five-, then a four-, and so forth, until somebody breaks the deadlock. As in "Jacks to Open," no player can use a passed turn to exchange letters from the tile bag during the prestart maneuvering.

The Auction Start

"The Auction Start" is admittedly gimmicky, but it can be fun in a four-handed social game. The same rules apply, as above, with the players agreeing in advance on the minimum length of the starting word. Say they agree on four letters. Probably three of them find they can make a four-letter word. The starter is then determined by each consecutive player calling out the first letter of the word he proposes to put down. If a player wishes to play cagey or cannot make a four-letter word, he may pass. The one with the highest starting letter gets the start and collects the double-word bonus. Incidentally, an alert player might deliberately call low and concede the start if he realizes he can capitalize on a previously announced letter and build a better-scoring word than if he started with a four-letter word of his own.

Ecology Scrabble

Ecology Scrabble has proved extremely popular because it brightens the game, increases the chance of seven-letter words, and introduces a poker-style constant "wild card" into play. I've dubbed it "Ecology Scrabble" because it involves recycling the blank.

Standard Scrabble rules apply until a blank is dropped on the board. Under basic rules the blank tile remains fixed to the board for the remainder of the game and represents whatever letter was designated by the player who placed it. In this variation any player can gain possession of the blank, providing it is his turn, by replacing it with a real letter that matches the original designation.

For example, if Player No. 1 places the word *paste* on the board and uses a blank for the letter *P*, then Player No. 2 can retrieve the blank by putting a real *P* in its place. The blank is then "clean" and can be used by Player No. 2 to represent any letter he chooses in a subsequent word. Switching a letter for a blank can only be done when it is a player's turn and does not constitute a move. Just because a player claims the blank, it does not force him to use it in the next turn, and he may hold it in his rack for as long as he wants before replaying it.

If a player chooses to "pass" on a turn and discard some of his letters, he is not entitled to claim the blank as part of that turn. In this variation both blanks can be used at least half a dozen times, and there is still room for strategy. Late in a game, a player can freeze the blank by dropping it and calling it some letter for which all tiles are already exposed on the board. For instance, the player who used the blank in the word *paste*, could have called the word *haste* and disabled the blank for the remainder of the game if both *H* tiles had been on the board. This strategy of neutering the blank becomes important in the final stages of the game.

Double Bag Scrabble

This is a variation for the people who complain that there are too many vowels in the Scrabble bag. In fact, there are 42 vowels and 56 consonants, but that is slight consolation for the player with a rackfull of *I*'s and *A*'s—especially if he does not know such vowel-consuming words as *aalii* and *riata*.

Scrabble Inventor Butts admits that one of the most frequent complaints about the game's structure is that there are too many tiles with the letter *I* on them. Butts said, "When I invented the game and was working out the tile distribution, I wanted to make sure I could get long words with the letters instead of a lot of little short words. The letter *I* is in there quite a lot because I like the endings you use like *ion* and *ing*. I also like to get words you can add prefixes and other suffixes to."

However, even Butts and his wife, Nina, it seems have become frustrated by the plethora of vowels in the game. Double Bag Scrabble is a game variation that Butts now plays regularly.

Before the game, you separate the vowels and consonants into two bags. At the start of play you are free to draw as many consonants or vowels as you like up to the regulation seven tiles. After a while, most people average out to four consonants and three vowels. Throughout the game you may restock your rack from either bag, which means that after each turn, you have to make a decision on which way to weight your hand.

The immediate reaction is to draw more heavily from the consonant bag to increase your chances of snaring high-scoring tiles like the *Z* and the *X*. Butts knocks that strategy down: "Drawing from the consonant bag all the time to get high-count letters won't do you any good unless you draw vowels to go with them. You'll find you have to draw from both bags, and in this variation you never get your hand lopsided."

One stipulation is that you must draw all your letters at once, such as two tiles from the consonant bag and immediately one from the vowel bag if you need three letters. It is illegal to draw several consonants, look at them, and then head for the vowels.

Double Bag Scrabble has become standard fare in the Butts household, and it was one variation Butts suggested to Jim Brunot for inclusion in the revised rules. "He didn't do anything with it, but he did send me a supply of those plastic tile bags, and I stuck my own labels on them marked 'vowels' and 'consonants' and gave them to friends."

Solitaire Scrabble

The game of Scrabble was designed for two, three, or four players, although it is best when played by two people. The fact that it is a game that can be played successfully by an odd number of competitors has always been a big selling point.

But a lot of people do not realize that you can also play an interesting game of Scrabble by yourself. I'll admit that when I first heard of Solitaire Scrabble, I was dubious. It seemed to me only human nature that I would cheat, maybe even subconsciously, when playing an imaginary opponent. I've since discovered, though, that Solitaire can be played honestly, and it can be exciting. It's great practice, and there's absolutely no pressure from an opponent on how much time you take per turn—hence more seven-letter words.

There are three variations of Solitaire Scrabble. One method is to play with a single rack of tiles, and instead of the average 15 turns in a game, you get more than 30. You play Standard Scrabble rules, keep restocking your rack, and take turn after turn. You keep a tally of your total game scores and each time try to improve on your best one.

The second method is to play with two racks and play against an imaginary opponent. The third method is to turn all the tiles face up on the table and, armed with a dictionary, deliberately try to build high-scoring words.

The best version, in my opinion, is the second one, played with two racks. To make it even more competitive, I have made the following refinements: After playing from rack No. 1, I do not immediately replenish it with tiles from the bag, but instead turn the depleted rack away from me and pick up rack No. 2. I then play rack No. 2 and turn it away without drawing fresh letters. Then I pick up rack No. 1, and only then do I draw the required letters from the tile bag to bring it back up to seven tiles. After playing rack No. 1 again, I turn it away, replenish rack No. 2, and play a word from it. If you delay the restocking process, there is always an element of doubt over what letters will be in the opposing rack when it comes time to play again.

I play this variation under basic Scrabble rules and play it as defensively as any normal hand—never setting up triple-word opportunities for the opposing hand. You can get so carried away in this game, looking for bingos, that you actually forget what letters are lurking in the other rack. And because you are playing yourself, the competition is pretty even, and the scores remain neck and neck.

The third version of playing with all tiles exposed on the table is a good vocabulary builder, but it is not as much fun and nowhere near as satisfying.

Theme Scrabble

Theme Scrabble refers to versions of the game where the only words permitted must pertain to a previously agreed upon theme. For example, if you decide politics is your game theme, then words used must be like *vote*, *elect, campaign, platform, poll,* and *candidate.* In post-Watergate days, presumably, you could also use words like *burglar, crook, bribe, bugger,* and, possibly, *expletive deleted.*

On Board No. 45 there is a game of Proper Name Scrabble, in which everything is featured from the Pittsburgh Steelers, to the nickname for the Boston Red Sox and TV Detective Kojak. *Case,* in this case, is Senator Clifford Case of New Jersey, and Pele is the soccer phenomenon.

You can play Baseball Scrabble, in which the names of any major league players are permitted as well as such obvious baseball terms as *strike, walk, bunt, slide, diamond,* and *base.* To make it easier, you can permit abbreviations such as *rbi* for "runs batted in" and such slang expressions as *ribby,* meaning the same thing.

Sexy Scrabble can be fun although I won't reproduce a sample game board here. Usually, in Dirty Scrabble or Sexy Scrabble, you are permitted to use any part of the body, all amorous words, and any expressions in the vernacular that you can get past your opponent.

In Hollywood Scrabble you are permitted to use the names of well-known actors, words from popular movie titles, plus such cinema words as *camera, dolly, zoom* (as in lens), *boffo, Oscar, sleeper,* and *flopperoo.*

Tee-are Urban, the man who owns and manufactures Scrabble in Australia, has several others, including Geography Scrabble, in which you can only use names of countries, cities, lakes, rivers, and so forth.

Obviously, the rules for Theme Scrabble are loose and consist of what you think is a fair thing at the time. The beauty of it, especially if four people are playing, is that you can take turns thinking up themes: there's Gourmet Scrabble, in which each word has to have something to do with the kitchen, or TV Scrabble, in which every word has to have a link to a TV show—or be a term used in the industry, such as the words *ratings, primetime, commercial,* or *network.*

Some of the most fun in these theme games is not the actual playing of a theme word but the often tortured reasoning by the player trying to get the word accepted. This applies, especially in Story Scrabble, in which each word played must continue on from the last played word to make a sentence.

Stopwatch Scrabble

This is the way the experts play the game. It's a clock-racing game for hotshots. It's the way I imagine chess whiz Bobby Fischer would play Scrabble. In this variation, literally every second counts and there is no room for the dodderer or the dawdler.

BOARD NO. 45

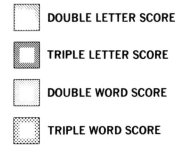

☐ DOUBLE LETTER SCORE

■ TRIPLE LETTER SCORE

☐ DOUBLE WORD SCORE

▨ TRIPLE WORD SCORE

Frank Kuehnrich, 1975 New York Scrabble champ, hates to play the game any other way; and if you play at a place like the Chess Center Game House on New York's West Seventy-Second Street, then this is the version to expect.

Shortly after winning his title against 850 opponents, Kuehnrich said, "Scrabble against the clock is the only way to play. Like in chess, you are given so many minutes per game to make your moves. It's up to the individual player to decide which moves are worth ten seconds of time and which moves are worth four minutes."

At the Chess Center, each player is permitted 15 minutes per game to make all his moves. He is also given a bonus three minutes to provide time for keeping score. That means each player has 18 minutes to complete his game, and it is up to each player to budget his time clock as he goes along. It averages out at about one minute a turn, there usually being between 15 and 18 moves per player in a two-man game. That doesn't mean, though, that each turn takes a minute. A player may take five minutes on a desperate gamble for a seven-letter drop and then sprint through later turns in seconds to balance his time clock.

There are two clocks alongside the board, and players stop and start their opponent's timepieces as in championship chess. The big difference is that in chess you lose if your clock runs out of time. In Stopwatch Scrabble you are still in the game if your 18 minutes runs out, but you are penalized 10 points for every minute you go over the limit.

□

This version of timed Scrabble should not be confused with Tournament Scrabble, in which each player is permitted a flat three minutes per turn to complete a move. If he fails to place a word in that time, the prerogative passes to his opponent, who also then starts a three-minute clock race. In tournament play it makes no difference if you drop one word in 10 seconds and a second word in 45 seconds and then are stumped on a hard one that makes your next three minutes run out. You can't "bank" time not used on a short turn.

Kuehnrich thinks this method is a foolish one. "Their system is wrong. The only way to time Scrabble is the same way as chess is timed. You get a set time for the complete game. Then it is up to you how much time you spend on individual moves. Some moves take seconds and others take minutes. To set an arbitrary three minutes per move is just wrong. The timing has to be organized so that it is the player's prerogative whether he spends a short time or a long time on a specific move."

For players who aren't in the 18-minute-a-game league, I suggest a 30-minute time limit. Then as you get better, you and your opponent can trim minutes from the time bank until you are down to the cutthroat level.

Anagram Scrabble

Players who enjoy deciphering anagrams or who play the syndicated newspaper game Jumble Words will enjoy Anagram Scrabble. Under this variation a player, when his turn comes, is permitted to rearrange any word on the board providing he meets two conditions. The first is that he add at least one more letter to the existing word, and the second is that the rearranged letters form an acceptable word and that interlocking words still make sense. The player then receives full credit for any new or altered words, but any previously covered premium letter and premium word squares are disregarded.

On Board No. 46 the Anagram Scrabbler attacks the word *navel* (*H* 11–15). He decides to rearrange that word and along the way picks up points for several other altered words and one new one.

On Board No. 47 he has added one letter, an *E*, and rearranged the letters so that they now extend from squares *H*–11 through *H*–15 and spell the word *leaven*. The word *vile* (15 *F–I*) has become *vine*, the word *bent* (11 *F–I*) has become *beet*, and the player has created a new two-letter word *lo* (10 *H–I*). He receives face value scores for all four words.

There is another version of Anagram Scrabble, which is a combination of Anagrams and Ecology Scrabble. It was developed by Robert Wood, Jr., of Princeton, New Jersey, and is designed to permit the repeated use of high-scoring letters.

At the start of his turn, a player may exchange any letter on the board for any letter in his hand, providing the transition leaves complete words on the board. Before laying down his own final word, he may make as many letter switches as he likes in a single turn, but he can only substitute one letter at a time, and each time the transaction must leave complete words on the board.

The player does not receive any points for these exchanges, but does have the advantage of gaining access to better letters, which are then counted in the usual way when he finally lays down his own word. By using this variation, players can get their hands on the big guns, the *Z*, *Q*, *X*, and *J*, several times in a game.

Foreign Scrabble

СКРЗБЛ О-Русски spells Scrabble in Russian Cyrillic letters. There are also editions in French, Italian, German, Spanish, Dutch, Arabic, and Swedish. Some people have even extracted the letters *K*, *Y*, *W*, and *Z* from their standard sets to play the game in Latin. Playing foreign

BOARD NO. 46

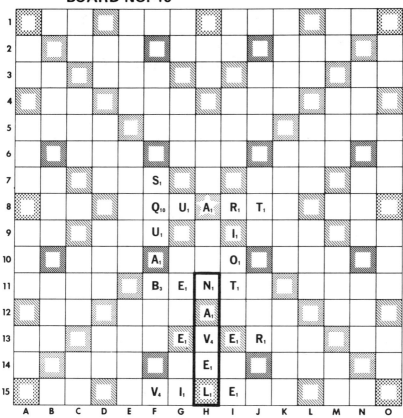

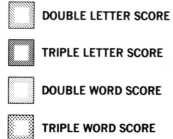 DOUBLE LETTER SCORE

TRIPLE LETTER SCORE

DOUBLE WORD SCORE

TRIPLE WORD SCORE

BOARD NO. 47

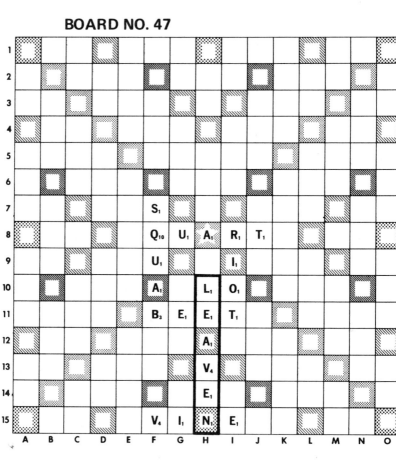

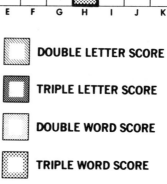

DOUBLE LETTER SCORE

TRIPLE LETTER SCORE

DOUBLE WORD SCORE

TRIPLE WORD SCORE

Scrabble, though, is not just a matter of switching languages—letter distributions have to be changed and tile values adjusted accordingly. In the Italian set, for example, letters like *K*, *W*, *X*, and *Y* are absent, and in the Dutch version of the game there are two letter *J* tiles instead of one, 10 *N* tiles instead of the standard six, and a total of 18 *E* tiles instead of 12.

The French Scrabble set does not have acute and grave accents on the *E* tiles, although there are more of them (15); the *Q* is worth only 8 points instead of regulation 10; the letter *M* is worth only 2 points instead of 3; and five letters—*W*, *X*, *Y*, *Z*, and *K*—are all worth 10 points each.

There is no *Y* in the German language, but there is a *Y* tile in German Scrabble. It makes German players adept at such foreign words as *yacht* and *yak*.

Foreign Scrabble is a great variation of the game if you are trying to learn a new language. Even if your vocabulary in that language is limited to three- and four-letter words, it is fun; and, more important for the language student, it forces you to think in the foreign language. It's no good thinking in English of the word *door*, for example, and then trying to translate it as *porte* in French.

Unscrabble

Fittingly, the last scrabble variation is Scrabble in reverse, a game called "Unscrabble." it was devised by a man named John Van Allen, of King's Beach, California, who is known in those parts as the "Tahoe Tinker."

Unscrabble is a perfect climax for one of those times when your board is crammed with brilliant words at the end of a normal game and you are reluctant to demolish it.

Unscrabble does ultimately clear the board, but does it with the finesse of a dainty eater. The procedure goes like this. The winner of the regular game removes at least one, but not more than six, tiles from the board. The tiles he lifts must all come from a single word on the board, and the letters he leaves behind must form complete words that, Scrabble style, properly connect with other words and lead back to the center star. Then the opponent plays. The game of Unscrabble ends when all the tiles have been removed from the board or a stalemate has developed where no more tiles can be removed without leaving incomplete words on the grid.

The game can be varied by changing the maximum number of removable letters in each turn. One way to do that is to roll dice, with each player being required to pick up the number of tiles shown on the dice roll.

There are two scoring systems for Unscrabble. The simplest is that each player receives face value for any letter he removes. The score can be added as you go along, or you can pile your plunder in front of you and total it up at the end. The second, more intricate scoring is to pay full value for premium letter and premium word squares. The bonuses are awarded to the player who uncovers the square concerned. As in real Scrabble, the bonuses can only be claimed once.

Part V

VOCABULARY

THE GREAT DICTIONARY
DISPUTE

'TWAS BRILLIG, AND THE SLITHY TOVES
DID GYRE AND GYMBLE IN THE WABE:
ALL MIMSY WERE THE BOROGOVES,
AND THE MOME RATHS OUTGRABE.
—*Lewis Carroll, on the death of the Jaabberwock in*
Through the Looking Glass

Carroll's warning to "beware the Jabberwock, my son," holds special meaning to the Scrabble player because this is one field in which Jabberwocks thrive. A cunning Jabberwock, with all his meaningless nonsense words, can hide all night behind the Tumtum tree.

One of the most difficult judgments in the game is to know when your opponent is indulging in Jabberwockery or when he actually has a legitimate word that only sounds like something out of Alice's Wonderland. For example, *bandersnatch* is Jabberwockery, but *bandicoot* is not.

Carroll's protagonist killed the Jabberwock with his "vorpal sword." Unfortunately, the only way a Scrabble player can dispatch his is to outgun him with his dictionary.

□

There are roughly 500,000 words in a normal unabridged English dictionary, and a reasonable vocabulary is 50,000 to 60,000 words. Our brains actually have the capacity to store all those half a million words plus every word in French, German, Chinese, and Swahili, but unfortunately most of us utilize only a fraction of our potential.

When it comes to Scrabble, a player with 75,000 words in his memory bank is going to start a game with an advantage over the player who has a mere 50,000. This does not mean, though, that the walking dictionary automatically is going to win—I've seen players with wide vocabularies beaten time and again by more limited opponents, who compensate with a flair for unscrambling anagrams and with a knack for tile placement.

The obvious solution is to build your word knowledge. Read a dictionary every day. That's what ex-Vice-President Spiro Agnew used to do. How else do you think he could come up with such expressions as "nattering nabobs of negativism"?

Just think of it: If you read, understand, and committed to memory 10 words a day, you would have 70 fresh words in your repertoire at the end of the first week and more than 3,600 new words hoarded away by the end of the year. And if, to start, you concentrated on good Scrabble words—the tricky, two-, three-, and four-letter ones containing high-scoring letters—then pretty soon your word arsenal would be heavily and impressively stocked.

This section contains tips on useful Scrabble words plus a few pointers on how to extend a reasonable word on the board into a better word and a rundown on those lucrative nuggets called seven-letter bingos. It also has a few words of warning about dictionary inconsistencies that can cost you a game unless you are fully aware of which dictionary is considered kosher in the house where the contest is being played.

For example, the word *ja* is permitted if you are playing with the *Funk & Wagnalls Standard College Dictionary.* It's listed as an interjection and an adverb meaning "yes" in German.

The Funk & Wagnalls was the official arbiter in the 1975 tournament play across the United States, and therefore *ja* was an important, strategic, two-letter word. In several other major dictionaries, however, including the unabridged Random House, it is listed in italics as a foreign word and is, therefore, banned. And in Webster's (unabridged) it is not listed at all except as an abbreviation for "joint account."

Here is another two-letter discrepancy. The word *te* is not permitted if you play by Funk & Wagnalls, but it is in Random House as an acceptable variation of the musical note *ti* on the diatonic scale.

Ironically, you are not even safe if you get hold of one of those Scrabble word guides, like the "authorized list" first published by Jacob Orleans and Edmund Jacobson back in 1953 when Scrabble was a new craze. If you try to play the word *zax* and then, when challenged, claim it appears three times in the word guide, you'd be right. But if you check the word guide's purported source, the Funk & Wagnalls, you'll find they've axed the *zax*. It still appears in Webster's and Random House as *zax*, a tool for trimming roofing slates, but in Funk & Wagnalls it is spelled only as *sax*. So you can see situations arising where the only way out is pistols at 20 paces.

□

Scrabble's producer and marketer, Jim Brunot, told me that dictionary squabbling was one thing he never dreamed of as an offshoot of the game. One thing that bugged him, especially, was the way the original rules were worded concerning foreign words.

"We said that any words were permitted if they were found in a standard dictionary except capitalized words and words designated as foreign words, then abbreviations, etc.," Brunot said. "We had more trouble with that 'designated foreign word' rule than anything else, I think. I wish we hadn't made that reference that way. "The dictionary I always played with back then used those two little parallel marks to distinctly stamp a word as foreign. There was no argument. Unfortunately, it differs so much now between dictionaries. Somebody, for example, plays the word for 'yes' in German, *ja*, and it's in the dictionary. Then somebody else says, 'Well, why can't I have *oui* for 'yes' in French?' Or Spanish for 'maybe.' It's a very frequent source of conflict." (Actually, *oui* is permissible as an adverb for "yes" in French in Funk & Wagnalls, and so is *si*, meaning "yes" in Portuguese, Italian, and Spanish.)

This is one of the reasons why Brunot claims to be more embarrassed than flattered when he meets people at cocktail parties and is introduced as "Mr. Scrabble." "People are always wanting to pick arguments about 'Is such and such a word?' It's almost unbelievable sometimes. We've had telephone calls from all over the country, from California, everywhere. They've come at all hours from people wanting me to be the arbiter on a challenged game."

Brunot always resisted the idea of having a standard dictionary as the Scrabble Bible, but on reflection said, "I suppose with a tournament you have to have one." He had need of one himself in a game several days before we talked at his winter retreat on Hilton Head Island in South Carolina.

"I was playing a friend," he recalled, "and she played the word *booted*. It was in a good position for me; so I played *unbooted* to extend it up to catch a triple-word square. She challenged me, and I knew I'd won, but unfortunately the dictionary I have here doesn't contain the word *unbooted*."

Despite his reputation for being a passive, gentlemanly Scrabble player, Jim Brunot is stubborn when he thinks he has been robbed. "I kept looking for that word," he said, "and I found it too. It was in the Oxford Dictionary, down at the local library. By then it was too late, of course. I'd been booted."

Which brings up the point of how does a word get into the dictionary in the first place?

□

Each time there is a major revision of a dictionary, the editors seek out new words and, often, new meanings for old words. New words come into use every day. Some are fad words that are coined to fit a political or social situation and then fade into oblivion. Some remain as part of the language even though their meaning may change drastically over the years.

The space race brought a welter of new words like *reentry, module, nose cone*, and *retro-rocket*. It also brought new meanings for old words like NASA's use of the word *nominal* to mean "Everything is going fine" and "anomalous when things are going disastrously.

The civil rights movement of the late 1950s and early 1960s brought the words *desegregation* and *sit-in* and gave the word *demonstration* an additional definition as a parade of protesters. The Vietnam War brought the overworked words *escalation* and *defoliation* and *preemptive* as in "preemptive reaction strike."

In politics came the words *détente, coexistence*, and *summitry*, and Richard Nixon's press secretary, Ron Ziegler, added such obfuscating gems as *inoperative*. In the recent vernacular the word *ball* came to mean "to have sexual intercourse," not "to dance," and, in reverse, the evolution of the word *jazz* changed it from a black expression meaning "to have intercourse" into a type of music. It's not that long ago that words like *transistorize* and *vaccinate* and *recyclable* and *introvert* and *overkill* and *biodegradable* were not in existence. And nobody knows how long *gay* will be accepted as meaning "homosexual" or if *swinger* will forever more be regarded as a definition of a person who engages in group sex.

Sidney Landau, former editor-in-chief at Funk & Wagnalls and currently editor-in-chief for a new Doubleday dictionary, said, "Until we have good grounds for believing that a particular term will remain in use for a number of years, we must postpone including it in the dictionary." He also said that all slang expressions, except the most common, were usually excluded from general dictionaries and so were the "most vulgar and taboo" expressions. In a booklet that Funk & Wagnalls published on the makeup of a dictionary, Landau said, "Dictionaries thus tend, however unintentionally, to act as a conservative influence on the language as a whole."

□

Once a word is selected for inclusion in the dictionary, it is then worked over by the dictionary staff, who will write the definition or definitions, and by the publishing house's panel of professors and English scholars. They check etymologies, the classification of terms (for example, informal, archaic, and so forth), pronunciations, and synonyms. Only then is the word ready for inclusion in the next revised edition of the big book.

To some people, a dictionary is a dictionary is a dictionary. As long as it is thick enough, it is bound to have nearly all the same words as a competitor. It may come as a surprise to people, but each dictionary does have its own style and flavor—even though lexicographers claim they strive to make the words used in describing each entry as explicit and as colorless as possible to avoid misinterpretation. For example, some American dictionaries are more liberal than others when it comes to English-English spellings and listings. It may be apocryphal, although perusal does seem to support the story, but there is a story that Funk & Wagnalls lists more Scottish words than any other dictionary because a top lexicographer there has a yen (or should I say ken) for things Scottish. Another explanation could be the fact that, according to Patrick Barrett, the *Standard College Dictionary* was designed to be especially attractive to the Canadian market, "so it has a collection of colloquialisms and dialect words of the United States and the British Isles."

□

Down at Scrabble headquarters, at 200 Fifth Avenue, New York City, they swear by the Funk & Wagnalls, at least until Scrabble's own dictionary comes out, because it is "the most eclectic dictionary around." But I have found, as I did recently with the word *poof*, that Webster's is the one to run to if all else fails.

I hope you can see after all this that a Scrabble house without a dictionary is a breeding ground for Jabberwocks. In fact, a game without a dictionary at hand can really put the "kaibosh" on a game.

And look *that* up in your Funk & Wagnalls.

21 TWO-LETTER WORDS

When you play Scrabble with the game's mentor, Alfred Butts, you get the impression that the original version of the game was meant for more genteel times. He permits the use of a dictionary to check spelling, "as long as you don't browse through it looking for words," and he doesn't like the tactic of using two-letter words as defensive strategy to keep the board tight. "I like to play an open game . . . to give everybody a chance to get their words down," he said.

Consequently, Butts does not place as much importance on the knowledge of two-letter words as tournament players do. For example, he did not know that the words *ma* and *pa* were acceptable, according to Funk & Wagnalls. "We'd never accept those," he said. "Anyway I don't accept Funk & Wagnalls. The one we use—in fact, the one we've used for years—is the Webster's unabridged. I wouldn't use anything else." (For the record both *ma* and *pa* are in Webster's.)

Despite Mr. Butts's sentiments, it is imperative that you recognize some of the odd two-letter words (including the word *od*) that are legal and can act as good hook-words for high-scoring bingos. If ever you doubt the clout of a two-letter word, remember the point made earlier in the book on how to use the single letter *X* to score 48 points.

According to most unabridged dictionaries, there are about 70 permissible two-letter words. In Funk & Wagnalls there are 69. Some good players know them all, and it is advisable to commit as many to memory as possible. If you can't memorize at least half of them, then at least scan the following list occasionally, and maybe a strange one, like *ex* or *ut*, will stick in your mind and surface as a winning play in a later game.

Another thing is that a player who knows a lot of these can often hoodwink a player who doesn't. After all, if you have been burned by challenging the word *ka,* which *is* a word, you might be reluctant to challenge *ko,* which is *not.*

These, then, are the most accepted two-letter words:

aa	ae	ai	an	as
ad	ah	am	ar	at

ax	er	if	ma	od	so
ay	en	in	me	on	ti
ba	ex	is	mi	or	to
be	fa	it	mu	os	up
by	go	ja	my	ox	us
de	ha	jo	na	pa	ut
do	he	ka	no	pe	we
eh	hi	la	nu	pi	wo
el	ho	li	of	re	xi
em	id	lo	oh	si	ye

One trap not to get into when playing two-letter words is to watch an opponent play the word *en* or *em* and then blithely assume that all letters in the alphabet can be used in that fashion. Not so. The words *en* and *em* *do* stand for those letters in the alphabet, but they also stand for printers' measures. Most letters of the alphabet, in fact, take phonetic three-letter spellings and are listed separately in the dictionary under *bee, cee, dee, eff, gee, jay, kay, ell* (also *el*), *pee, are, ess, tee, vee,* and *ex.* The vowels and the *Y* are spelled as they look, and so are the *Q* (also *cue*) and the *W,* surprisingly enough, although the *W* can also be spelled *doubleyou.* The letter *H* forms a good word, *aitch,* and so does the *Z,* which can be spelled either as *zee* or with the English-English spelling and pronunciation *zed*.

Once you have memorized these, you have a great source of short words for plurals. For example, the plural of the letter *Q,* as in "Mind your *p*'s and *q*'s," can be spelled with the apostrophe or simply as *qs,* according to some major dictionaries.

That ploy is not listed in the preceding list of two-letter words because the whole idea of using letters of the alphabet is often disputed, let alone pluralizing them. In Tournament Scrabble you are not allowed to use *qs* or *ws* or *cs* as the plural of a letter of the alphabet, and some house rules have a blanket ban on letters of the alphabet—whether they be *qs,* aitches, or betas.

If you want to play strictly by the book, though, the dictionary does list "*qs*—plural of *q*" as well as "*ws*" as plural of *w* and "*ys*" as a version of the plural of the letter *y*. The *y* plural can also be spelled *wyes.* The plural for the letter *o* appears as *os* or *oes*—take your pick—and *x* becomes *exes.* In the case of the letter *z,* I can literally say it is last but not least. The last letter in the alphabet has four plural variations. They are *z*'s, *zs, zees,* and *zeds.*

This whole argument, though, is one that must be settled amicably, I hope, in individual households.

Once you have etched the two-letter tricksters in your mind, it is time to tackle the three-letter words. And what better, or more orderly, place to start than with three-letter words, which can be made by adding a single letter to a two-letter word already on the board?

A large repertoire of these words is a great Scrabble asset—especially when you are angling for the 50-point bonus that a seven-letter bingo brings. The reason is simple. Often opponents won't leave an easy opening for a seven-letter drop. They'll deliberately shut off an exposed *S* or an exposed *D* or *T*. Yet they will blindly leave the word *ha* exposed for you, and you can tag a *J* on to it to make the three-letter word *haj* going horizontally and a bingo word like *jodhpur* going vertically.

Some of these two-into-three words are obvious—words like *at* or *in* being transformed into *bat, cat, fat, hat,* or *bin, tin, kin,* or *win* by merely adding a letter up front. And by placing a letter on the tail, words like *ho* or *ba* can easily be extended into *hob, hop, hog,* and *hod* or *baa, bag, bay,* or *bas.* The ones to remeber, though, are the obscure ones—like putting an *M* after the word *is* to make *ism* or a *Z* in fron of *ax* to make *zax.*

The following are a few unusual three-letter words that can be formed by adding a single letter to an acceptable two-letter word already on the board. The new letter is added in front in some words and at the rear on others.

ADD AN A:

aba	ala	ane
aby	ama	goa
baa	ami	ani
ain	amu	
ait	ana	

ADD A B:

baa	bey	kab
bah	bis	nob

bel	bye	mib
ben		

ADD A C:

cam	cox	orc
cay	lac	

ADD A D:

dor	eld	yod
dup	tod	

ADD AN E:

axe	eel	hie
ane	eme	mae
dee	joe	ode
		kae

ADD AN F

fax	fid	fas
fen	foh	fon
		off

ADD A G:

gad	gar	mig
gae	jag	mag
gid	nog	teg
		erg

ADD AN H:

hae	hod	noh
hid	hex	

ADD AN I:

ami	ani	rei

ADD A J:

jow	jus	haj

ADD A **K**:

kae	kor	kex
ken	kas	kay

ADD AN **L**:

aal	las	mel
bel	lar	mil
dol	lex	til

ADD AN **M**:

mae	mut	rem
mho	nom	tom
mon	pam	mas
		ism

ADD AN **N**:

nae	ben	yon
noh	wen	

ADD AN **O**:

obe	ope	loo
oka	too	noo
		oho

ADD A **P**:

pam	psi	yep
pas	pye	pax
phi	wop	pox

ADD A **Q**:
nil

ADD AN **R**:

rax	rin	tor
rem	dor	mir
rex	lar	rad

ADD AN S:

ays	kas	˙sen
mas	las	sax
		sex

ADD A T:

tae	tho	tup
tam	tor	ait
het	ort	wot

ADD A U:

udo	amu	piu
uit	emu	

ADD A V:

vas	vis	rev
vex	vox	dev
vin	von	

ADD A W:

wae	wye	yew
wat	jaw	wen
maw	wha	wis

ADD AN X:

pix	six	lax
pax	sox	mix

ADD A Y:

bey	hoy	yod
kay	yin	yon
yow	dey	

ADD A Z:

adz
zax

Once you get into the thought channel of automatically seeing word extensions, even by one letter in either direction, it's not long before you start exploiting two-letter words by extending them from both ends in a single turn. Then you can seize on an exposed *ai* and jump on both ends with your seven tiles to make a word like *m–ai–lboxes* for a bingo. Or the previously mentioned *j–od –hpur*, which wouldn't be a bingo, but would still give you a healthy score.

Three-letter words that don't originate from two-letter ones are also of prime importance in Scrabble—especially the ones with high-scoring consonants like *fez* and *qua* and *pyx*. The following is a list of some good ones, not all of them by any means:

aga	ell	lea
alp	fet	lev
auk	feu	lum
ava	fey	lux
ave	fez	moa
awa	fiz	mol
awn	fob	mot
azo	foy	mun
bee	ged	nix
bot	gee	nth
bur	gey	obi
cee	gib	oot
cos	gie	ose
coz	gip	oui
dee	gyp	poi
dag	het	pur
dak	jee	pyx
dap	jeu	pee
daw	jew	qua
duc	kay	quo
eau	kea	raj
ecu	kef	sab
edh	kep	sal
eft	kip	sec
ern	kop	syn
eta	kos	tun
eth	leu	
eff		

twa	vet	wiz
ugh	voe	yuk
	vug	
vau	wab	zoa
vee	wap	zee
vav	wop	zed
vaw		

23 FOUR-, FIVE-, AND SIX-LETTER WORDS

It is conceivable, though I've never seen anyone do it, for a player to complete a 15-letter word on a single play. In theory, a player could thread his seven letters through a patchwork of letters already on the board and wind up with a 15-letter epic like *equiponderating* (the art of counterbalancing). For argument's sake, assume that the bottom row on the board reads – – – – – *ON* – – *RATING*, and this lucky hypothetical player happens to have the letters *P,D,Q,U,I,E,I,E* on his rack and the word *equiponderating* in his head.

I mention this remote possibility to illustrate the endless combinations imaginable in Scrabble and to explain why, in this chapter, I make no attempt to list all four-, five-, and six-letter words available. For that, you would have to staple a dictionary on the back of this book.

Instead, I have concentrated on the big four—the Z, Q, X, and J. They are the most profitable tiles because they have the highest point value and are the hardest to place. There is only one of each in the 100 tiles, and unless you are playing Ecology Scrabble, where letters are recycled, they come round only once in a game.

Although the number of words with a Z or a Q in them is limited, such words are not *that* scarce, and no player should shy away from them. In fact, once you have memorized a few words like *zloty* and *quezal* and *phlox* and *jonquil*, you relish the times when your groping fingers pull one of this quartet from the tile bag.

The following word lists contain some of the more rewarding, unusual words using the big four.

Some of the words listed use the main letter more than once, like *hajj* or *huzza*, which would eliminate them unless a player has a blank as well. The list is by no means complete, and all obvious words like *daze*, *doze*, *freeze*, or *breeze* have been omitted. Only where a word has a tricky alternate spelling is it included.

FOUR-LETTER WORDS WITH A **Z**:

adze	dozy	hazy
azym	friz	jazz
czar	fuzz	mazy

oozy	vizy	zeta
oyez	whiz	zoic
sizz	zebu	zoon
tzar	zein	zyme

FOUR-LETTER WORDS WITH A **Q**:

quad	quay	quiz
quag	quid	quod

FOUR-LETTER WORDS WITH AN **X**:

apex	flax	moxa
axil	flux	nixy
axis	ibex	oryx
axle	ilex	pixy
axon	ixia	sext
coxa	jinx	taxa
doxy	lynx	xyst
eaux	minx	

FOUR-LETTER WORDS WITH A **J**:

hadj	jarl	jowl
haje	jazz	juba
haji	jess	jube
hajj	jill	juju
jady	jinn	jura
jamb	jinx	jute
jape	jole	raja
jark	joll	

FIVE-LETTER WORDS WITH A **Z**:

azoic	croze	izzat
azote	dizen	jazzy
azure	fizzy	kazoo
azyme	frizz	lazar
bazar	furze	mazer
bezel	furzy	mezzo
bonze	fuzee	mirza
bortz	fuzil	mizen
braza	fuzzy	oryza
braze	gauzy	ozena
colza	hazel	ozone
cozen	huzza	ouzel

razee	winze	zloty
sizar	wizen	zombi
sozin	zamia	vizzy
spitz	zayin	zooid
topaz	zebec	zoril
vizir	zibet	
vizor	zinky	

FIVE-LETTER WORDS WITH A Q

fique	quern	quirt
pique	queue	quoin
quaff	quill	quoit
quail	quilt	quoth
qualm	quint	roque
quash	quipu	squab
quean	quire	toque
querl	quirl	tuque

FIVE-LETTER WORDS WITH AN X:

addax	exult	oxyde
admix	flaxy	phlox
affix	galax	pulex
annex	helix	pyxie
ataxy	hexad	pyxis
axial	hexyl	radix
axile	hyrax	remex
axiom	infix	silex
axled	ixtle	taxad
axone	kylix	unsex
beaux	latex	varix
borax	laxly	xebec
boxen	malax	xenia
braxy	maxim	xenon
buxom	murex	xerus
calix	nixie	xylan
calyx	noxal	xylem
cimex	oxbow	xylic
codex	oxeye	xylol
coxae	oxime	xylyl
cylix	oxlip	xysti
excel		

FIVE-LETTER WORDS WITH A J:

bijou	jazzy	jugal
ejido	jebel	julep
fjord	jehad	jumbo
hadji	jemmy	junco
hadjj	jenny	junta
jabot	jerry	jupon
jacal	jihad	jural
jacko	jimmy	jurat
jacky	jinni	jutty
jaggy	jinny	mujik
jakes	jocko	rajah
jalap	joram	sajah
jambe	jorum	slojd
jaspe	jougs	thuja
	joule	

SIX-LETTER WORDS WITH A Z:

ablaze	evzone	piazza
assize	fizgig	pizzle
azalea	foozle	podzol
azonal	frazil	quezal
azonic	frieze	razzia
azotic	frizer	seizor
azymus	frowzy	sleazy
benzin	gazebo	stanza
benzol	guzzle	syzygy
benzyl	huzzah	teazel
bezant	izzard	touzle
bezoar	mazily	towzle
blazon	mizpah	tweeze
blazer	mizzen	tzetze
blowzy	mizzly	vizard
bonzer	muzhik	vizier
borzoi	muzjik	wheeze
bronzy	nyanza	zaffar
chintz	ozaena	zaffer
coryza	ozoena	zaffir
crozer	ozonic	zaffre
eczema	panzer	zareba

zebeck	zinnia	zonule
zechin	zircon	zoonal
zenana	zither	zorila
zephyr	zombie	zounds
zeugma	zonary	zygoma
zinced	zonate	zygote
zincky	zonula	zymase

SIX-LETTER WORDS WITH A Q:

barque	piquet	quinic
basque	pulque	quinin
bisque	quaere	quinsy
caique	quagga	quohog
cinque	quaggy	risque
cirque	quahog	roquet
claque	qualmy	sacque
cliquy	quanta	squail
coquet	quarte	squama
maquis	quarto	squill
masque	quezal	toquet
mosque	quince	torque

SIX-LETTER WORDS WITH AN X:

adieux	diplex	oxalic
admixt	duplex	oxalis
afflux	efflux	oxymel
ataxia	elixir	paxwax
ataxic	extant	phenix
axilla	fixate	pickax
axseed	fixity	plexor
biaxal	flexor	plexus
bijoux	galaxy	pollex
bombyx	hallux	praxis
calxes	hexane	prolix
caudex	hexone	reflux
coaxal	larynx	scolex
coccyx	luxate	sextan
commix	matrix	sexton
cortex	maxima	spadix
cruxes	maxixe	storax
dexter	meninx	syntax
dioxid	orexis	syrinx

taxine	turnix	xyloid
taxite	vertex	xylose
thorax	vortex	xyster
toxine	xylene	xystus

SIX-LETTER WORDS WITH A **J**:

abjure	jarabe	jocund
acajou	jarfly	joseph
bijoux	jarina	jounce
crojik	jasper	jubate
donjon	jejune	jugate
frijol	jennet	jujube
hadjee	jerboa	jungly
hejira	jereed	jurane
jabber	jerkin	jurant
jacana	jetton	moujik
jackey	jigget	muzjik
jadish	jingal	swaraj
jaeger	jinnee	wejack
	jocose	

24 SEVEN-LETTER "BINGO" WORDS

When Jim Brunot took over Alfred Butts's game and changed its name from Criss-crosswords to Scrabble, he changed very little else. He did have one innovation, however, that drastically altered the scoring system for the game and also totally changed some competitors' style of play.

Brunot decreed that if you successfully laid down all seven letters in your rack in a single turn, you were entitled to a bonus of 50 points on top of the points you would normally score for that play. Such a move, often a game-winning one, has been called a lot of different things, not all of them flattering, over the years. Brunot called it a "fifty-point premium word." I have alternately referred to it as a "seven-letter drop," "a boardbuster," a "sweep," or a "slam" and by the English tag, "a Scrabble." For a while I considered calling it a "brunot" in honor of the man who invented the bonus. The Tournament Scrabble people call it a "bingo"—an expression loathed by the game's inventor, Butts, because it sounds as if it has been stolen from a certain other board game. But it has been through Tournament Scrabble that the seven-letter play has been perfected. So "bingo" it is.

The bingo game, how and when to play it, is detailed with all its heroics and heartbreaks in the strategy part of the book. What follows here is a list of key word endings, common prefixes, seven-letter words containing the "big four" letters, and a rundown on the "satire syndrome" —a tricky code to smoke well-hidden bingos out of your rack.

□

To start, the most common source of bingos is to be found in the following word endings: -ies, -ing, -ent, -ble, -iest, -ed, -ter. Other endings that give you a good leg up toward a bingo word are -ion, -tion, -tian, -cing, -able, -ment.

The endings er and est are the most commonly used in the English language for comparatives and superlatives. For example: cold, colder, coldest. This form of word ending is so common that most general dictionaries do not even include it. If a listed word has a normal declension, then *er* and *est* are taken for granted as the comparative and superlative forms. If the word ending is unusual—like *happy, happier, happiest*—then it will be specifically noted. And it will also be listed if the word changes completely like *bad, worse, worst*.

A good Scrabble player also knows common prefixes like *un-, re-, mis-, inter-*, and so on.

Some letters combine easily with each other to make seven-letter words whereas others are as compatible as oil and water. That is where the "satire syndrome" comes in. A few years ago somebody came across the fact that the six-letter word *satire* is one of the most promiscuous words in the language—it will mate with practically any other letter to form a seven-letter bingo. As a matter of fact, as noted earlier, if you add any one of 18 of the 26 letters in the alphabet to the letters in the word *satire*, you'll get a bingo word. At tournaments across the United States, players use the *satire* test along with several others like *retina* and *santer*, and New York's 1975 champion, Frank Kuehnrich, admitted to using the *satire* system as well as several other six-letter yardsticks of his own that he was determined to keep to himself.

□

Sometimes, though, slavish devotion to these key combinations, coupled with a faulty memory, can bring on an acute attack of nail-biting. In one dismal game, in which I was soundly thrashed, I suddenly found the magic letters S,A,T,I,R,E hidden in my jumbled rack. The seventh letter was an O. I ran my time out in a futile letter-shuffling attempt to find the elusive word. Later I checked and found that the letter O is one of the eight letters that does *not* combine with *satire* for a bingo.

Using *satire* as a building block, you can make a fistful of "bingo" words by the addition of a single letter. Here are 52 of them:

A — aristae
B — baiters, terbias, barites
C — raciest, stearic
D — tirades, staider, astride, disaster, disrate
E — seriate
F — fairest
G — stagier, gaiters, seagirt, aigrets
H — hastier
I — airiest
J — nil
K — nil

L — retails, slatier, realist, saltire, saltier
M — imarets, misrate
N — retains, stainer, nastier, ratines, retinas, stearin, restain
O — nil
P — parties, traipse, pastier, pirates, piaster
Q — nil
R — tarries, tarsier
S — satires
T — ratites, tastier, artiste, striate, attires
U — nil
V — veritas, vastier
W — wastrie, wariest, watiers, waister
X — nil
Y — nil
Z — nil

□

The stock letters forming the word *retina* can be teamed with 16 other letters to make a word; in this case, 45 words:
A — nil
B — nil
C — certain, creatin
D — detrain, trained
E — trainee, retinae
F — fainter
G — ingrate, granite, tangier, tearing
H — nil
I — inertia, inearth
J — nil
K — keratin
L — latrine, retinal, reliant, trenail, ratline
M — raiment, minaret
N — entrain
O — nil
P — pertain, painter, repaint
Q — nil
R — trainer, retrain, terrain
S — stainer, nastier, retinas, retains, ratines, stearin
T — nitrate, tertian, nattier, tainter
U — ruinate, urinate, uranite, taurine
V—nil

W — tawnier, tinware
X — nil
Y — nil
Z — nil

☐

Under the same system, the word *santer*, although unacceptable when standing alone, combines with 18 letters for 44 bingo words:

A — nil
B — banters
C — trances, canters, scanter, nectars, recants
D — stander
E — earnest, nearest, eastern
F — nil
G — strange, garnets, argents
H — thenars, anthers
I — nastier, retains, stainer, retinas, stearin
J — nil
K — tankers, rankest
L — sternal, antlers, saltern
M — smarten, martens
N — tanners
O — treason, senator, roanest, atoners
P — parents, arpents, trepans, pastern
Q — nil
R — ranters
S — nil
T — tatters
U — saunter, natures
V — taverns, versant, servant
W — wanters
X — nil
Y — nil
Z — nil

☐

With words like *trepans*, *stearin*, *terbias*, and *striate*, you may think that you'll never shake a bingo from your hand.

However, if you are not yet totally discouraged, then the following list of other bingo combinations might be of interest. As in the chapters on useful three-, four-, five-, and six-letter words, the list is restricted to unusual words, utilizing the Z, Q, X, and J.

SEVEN-LETTER WORDS WITH A Z

alcazar	diazole	zacaton
apprize	dozenth	zaptiah
azimuth	ebonize	zaptieh
azotise	elegize	zareeba
azurite	emblaze	zebrass
azygous	fuzzily	zebrine
bazooka	gizzard	zebroid
benzene	lazaret	zebrula
benzine	matzoon	zebrule
benzoic	matzoth	zecchin
benzoin	mazurka	zedoary
benzoyl	mestiza	zemstvo
bezique	mezuzah	zeolite
blowzed	mitzvah	zincate
britzka	muezzin	zincify
bromize	obelize	zincing
buzzwig	oxazine	zincite
canzone	ozonide	zincked
canzoni	ozonize	zincous
chintzy	ozonous	zingara
coenzym	peptize	zingaro
cognize	quetzel	zittern
cozener	rhizoid	zoisite
crozier	rhizoma	zooidal
cruzado	rhizome	zoonomy
cyanize	scherzo	zootomy
czardom	scherzi	zygosis
czarina	squeeze	zymogen
czarism	swizzle	zymosis
diazine	tzarina	zymotic
		zymurgy

SEVEN-LETTER WORDS WITH A Q:

aliquot	cliquey	equerry
aquaria	coequal	jonquil
aqueous	coquina	lacquer
briquet	cumquat	liquefy
cacique	equable	marquee

marquis	quassin	racquet
masquer	quayage	relique
obloquy	querist	requiem
obsequy	quetzel	ronquil
oquassa	quiddle	rorqual
parquet	quietus	sequela
pasquil	quillai	sequent
pasquin	quilter	sequoia
picquet	quinary	siliqua
piquant	quinate	silique
quadrat	quinine	squabby
quadric	quinnat	squally
quaffer	quinoid	squamae
quamash	quinone	squatty
quantic	quintal	squalch
quantum	quintan	squinch
quartan	quittor	squilla
quassia	quondam	squirmy

SEVEN-LETTER WORDS WITH AN X:

anthrax	foxbane	peroxid
apyrexy	foxfire	phalanx
axillae	foxfish	pickaxe
axillar	foxskin	pyrexia
axolotl	hexadic	pyrexic
biaxial	jackbox	radixes
boxhaul	lexical	salpinx
bureaux	lexicon	saxhorn
cachexy	maxilla	saxtuba
carapax	maximal	sextile
chevaux	maxwell	simplex
coaxial	mixible	synaxis
conflux	noxious	taxicab
coxcomb	overtax	taxitic
dextral	oxazine	tectrix
dioxide	oxidase	textual
expiate	oxidate	toxemia
expunge	oxyacid	toxemic
flexile	oxyntic	toxical
flexion	oxysalt	trioxid
flexure	oxytone	triplex
fluxion	pemphix	xanthic

xanthin   xerotic   xylidin
xerosis   xiphoid

SEVEN-LETTER WORDS WITH A J:

abjurer   jaggery   jonquil
adjudge   jalapin   jugular
adjunct   jambeau   jujitsu
adjurer   jargoon   juniper
basenji   jejunum   junkman
cajeput   jeofail   juridic
conjoin   jewfish   juryman
disject   jingall   jussive
frijole   jobbery   mojarra
jacinth   jollity   sapajou
jackdaw   jasmine   sejeant
jackleg   jessant   sjambok
jaconet   jinglet   subjoin
jadeite   joinder   traject

25 THE WORD DUMP

You don't have to know that *cooee* is an Australian bushman's shout to attract somebody's attention or that a *hoopoo* is a dazzlingly plumed European bird. But if you want to be a good Scrabble player, you *do* have to know that *cooee* and *hoopoo* are indeed legitimate words and are an essential part of Scrabble vocabulary.

Such vowel-crammed words are known as "dumpers" in the Scrabble business. They are words you pull out of your stockpile when your rack is vowel-heavy and when you don't want to miss a turn by passing in order to get rid of the often duplicated, offending tiles. After all, unless you know about that hoopoo bird, you could be in trouble with a rack of tiles containing the letters *P,H,O,O,O,O*.

In the strategy part of the book, I discussed rack balancing and the tactic of "dumping." Here, then, are a few good dumpers to help you play your way out of trouble rather than forfeit a turn by passing.

aalii	ciliae	idiom
aculei	cooer	iota
adieu	donee	ionic
aerie	eerie	ileac
aoudad	eerily	iguana
apogee	eyrie	lanai
aquose	epopee	luau
audio	epopoeia	melee
aural	emeu	miaou
aureous	epee	oleate
aurora	etwee	oleo
bureau	fiancée	oriole
balata	guaiac	ovaria
baboo	heaume	ovolo
beau	hoodoo	oribi
cooee	hoopoe	oolite
cilia	hoopoo	ooglea

oogloea	raia	taboo
paleae	radii	tiara
peewee	radio	unau
piano	ratio	voodoo
queue	roue	wahoo
quaere	souari	

26 SWITCH-HITTERS

Scrabble is a game in which the old adage about "a bird in the hand" is not necessarily true. A bird in the hand, or should I say a word in the hand, is not always worth two in the bush.

The problem for some players is to shake the branches hard enough to dislodge the other hidden words—words that use identical letters to the one originally chosen but which can be worth more points. For example, I have the bingo word *reverse* in my hand. I'm so elated at getting a 50-point bonus that I look no further. But the letters that comprise the word *reverse* also make up the word *reserve*, and there is a chance that by going for the second option, the letter *V* may land on a triple-letter score for 12 points instead of the *S*, which would only be worth 3 points. You may think that the difference of 9 points is miniscule when compared to the 60-plus points you score for the bingo. Just remember it, though, when you lose a game by 8 points. That word *reverse*, incidentally, also makes the word *severer*.

Switch-words give you more freedom when you are looking for spots on the board to attach your words, and often a variation is worth more points. You have the word *faster* in your hand and think how great it would be if it ended in an *E* because you have spotted a prime square to extend a previously played word with an *E*. Well, *faster* also spells *strafe* if you take some time and shuffle your tiles thoroughly enough.

Some of these "switch-hitters," especially the longer ones, were listed in the chapter on seven-letter words. The ones following here are some common, shorter ones that may help your game:

    ache, each
    abets, beats, beast, baste, bates
    aids, said, dias
    ales, sale, seal
    amen, name, mane, mean
    arid, raid
    aster, rates, stare, tares, tears
    angel, angle, glean
    ascot, coast
    aside, ideas

beard, bared, bread
below, bowel, elbow
brief, fiber
browse, bowers
bleats, stable, tables

crapes, recaps, spacer, pacers, capers, scrape
cause, sauce
chaste, cheats, scathe
cheater, teacher
cited, edict
coax, coxa
corset, sector
crisp, scrip
cartel, claret
coins, icons, scion, sonic

dare, dear, read
daze, adze
dealer, leader, redeal
draws, sward, wards
detail, dilate, tailed
drapes, parsed, spader, spared, spread
denied, indeed
dale, deal, lade, lead
diet, edit, tide, tied

earth, heart, hater
east, eats, seat, seta, etas
emit, mite, item, time
ether, there, three

fares, fears, safer
filed, field, flied
filer, flier, rifle, lifer
finger, fringe
faster, strafe

girth, right
granite, tearing
groan, organ, orang
glare, large, regal, lager

hares, hears, share, shear
hewn, when

horse, hoser, shore
hinge, neigh

inks, skin, kins, sink
itself, stifle, filets
inert, inter, niter, nitre, trine

jar, raj, ajar, raja
jaunt, junta

kale, leak

laces, scale
lame, male, meal
leap, pale, peal, plea
limes, miles, smile, slime
lose, loes, sloe, sole
lilts, still

mate, meat, team, tame
meteor, remote

notes, onset, seton, stone, tones
night, thing

ought, tough
orts, rots, sort, tors

parts, strap, traps, sprat
pines, spine, snipe
paws, swap, wasp
pares, pears, reaps, rapes, spare
pest, pets, step
paste, spate, pates, tapes
pores, poser, prose, ropes, spore

quote, toque
quiet, quite

rats, tars, star
respect, spectre, sceptre, scepter
reserve, reverse, severer

saint, satin, stain
sheet, these
skate, stake, steak, teaks, takes

tires, tries, rites

tens, nets, sten, sent
torque, roquet

unite, untie
use, sue
unhat, haunt

veal, vale
vase, save
vee, eve

when, hewn
wont, town
weld, lewd
wards, sward, draws
wider, weird
went, newt

yard, dray
yak, kay

27 PLURALS

Some memorable arguments have erupted at my Scrabble table—as I'm sure they have at yours—by unusual attempts to transform words already on the board. On occasion, our games have stalled for interminable periods while wrangling went on over somebody's attempt to change a verb into a noun—like extending the word *exile* into *exiler* or *braid* into *braider.*

Both those examples, incidentally, are legal, and making nouns out of verbs is a field worth tilling. A nailer is one who nails, a hammerer is one who hammers, and if a cutter is one who cuts, then equally justifiable is a sawer for one who saws or a hacker for one who hacks.

But the longest, most vociferous, and most intense arguments I have found have usually concerned the pluralization of words. When can you add an S or ES to an existing word and legally pluralize it? The answer, if it is a noun, is: almost always.

There are some people, including lexicographers, who believe that any word in the language can be pluralized. For example, the word *pink* is an adjective, yet it can be used as a noun and used in a sentence like this—"The house painter came with a selection of paint samples. He had four varieties of brown, five pinks, three reds, and a yellow."

The word *if* is a conjunction, but it can be pluralized "without any ifs or buts." Patrick Barrett, lexicographer at Funk & Wagnalls, pluralized *if* for me in another context: "I have checked the above page and find six ifs in it." Barrett also acknowledges the argument that, possibly, all words can be pluralized, but said, "That really opens a can of worms."

☐

To me the question of when is a plural not a plural will always be known as "the great veal debate." Two friends, who shall remain nameless, were locked in a tight game and Player No. 1 put down the word *veal.* Player No. 2 added an S to make it *veals,* grabbing a triple-word score bingo plus the lead. The word was challenged, and the challenge triggered an argument that has simmered ever since.

Player No. 1 was right. The word *veals*, plural of *veal*, was not in the dictionary. But then nouns that take standard plural forms, an *s* or an *es*, are never spelled out in dictionaries for space reasons.

Webster's supported Player No. 2. On the subject of plurals, it said: "The plurals of English nouns are regularly formed in writing by the suffixation of the letter *s* (*hat–hats*) or the letters *es* (*cross–crosses*)."

Webster's next spelled out how plurals were pronounced and then said: ". . . although there are many exceptions to be noted, this regularity is so dominant that in theory all English nouns may be said to be capable of an analogical plural in the letters *-s* or *-es* and in practice little hesitation in so forming a new or unknown plural should be felt."

Back to the word *veals*. According to Webster's, *veal* is a noun meaning "a small calf." It is also the flesh of a calf from a few days to 12 to 14 weeks old. It is also a verb—to veal—meaning "to kill or dress a calf for veal." Therefore, *veal* (the flesh) cannot be pluralized, but *veal* (the beast) can.

The discussion between the two players in this story led to questions over whether, if veal can be pluralized, you can have *beefs* and *porks*. In the case of beefs, the answer is "Yes" with a qualification. The plural of *beef* (meaning "an adult cow, steer, or bull") is *beeves*. When *beef* means a complaint, then the plural is beefs.

Beef, the flesh, like *veal*, the flesh, is already pluralized. And so is pork. The only way *pork* can be pluralized is when it's a porker and there is enough meat in that for continuing the argument.

I mention this at length because it is indicative of the type of argument that crops up again and again. There are three things to remember:

1. Most nouns can take an *s* or *es* as a plural and, as Webster's puts it, you should show "little hesitation" in doing so even if the plural is "new and unusual."

2. Just because a plural is not in the dictionary does not mean it is illegal. If the word *dog* is there, but the word *dogs* is not, there is no logic in demanding that *veals* should be.

3. If the pluralization is extraordinary (for example, *beeves*), it will be listed the same way that *mouse* and *mice* are or *deer* and *deer*. (*Deers* is also acceptable.)

Part VI

SCRABBLE TRIVIA

In researching this book, I came up with an alphabet soup bowl full of factual and fictional morsels that have helped build a legend around the game of Scrabble. For example, did you know that the game's inventor, Alfred Butts, often gets beaten by his wife, Nina, because he is (to put it politely) "an indifferent speller"?

And did you know that way back before it became known as Scrabble, the game bore a name that was created when Butts punned his own first name? He called his game "Alph." I know that's true because I've seen an old board with the name "Alph" stenciled on it.

It is not true, however, that the American composer-conductor Leonard Bernstein once had a thousand-dollar, customized, monogrammed Scrabble set made out of ivory. Bernstein, who has no idea how the persistent rumor started, hasn't played Scrabble for years and claims his favorite word game is Anagrams. And it is also false that the *Guinness Book of Records* lists a marathon game of underwater Scrabble played with lead-weighted board and tiles on the bottom of a swimming pool. That was Monopoly.

Anyway, what follows here are a few Scrabble myths and milestones and other Scrabble trivia. They may be of no earthly use to you, except perhaps to psyche out an opponent with a casual, "Did you know that ..." just before the start of a game.

□

Although underwater Scrabble does not get a mention in the *Guinness Book of Records*, a dry-land marathon game does. At 10:15 A.M. on April 14, 1973, four students in Lakewood, California, started a Scrabble-athon. Playing in shifts, with a maximum break of 30 minutes uninterrupted sleep, Mike Borello, Mike Wilson, Rick Varga, and Pat Edmond Scrabbled for more than four days. They ceased play after 100 hours, during which time 20 games were completed. Their final cumulative scores were: Borello, 2,854; Wilson, 2,133; Varga, 1,902; and Edmond, 1,828.

That Californian effort has already been bettered. On August 31, 1975, four Australian Scrabbleniks, playing in a store window in downtown Sydney, set a new, unofficial, record of 120 hours. The men, all employees of the Overseas Telecommunications Commission, took aim at the Americans' record to raise money for the O.T.C. entrant in the Miss Australia quest. The quartet consisted of Mark Morris, 31, Jean-Pierre Burdinat, 21, Robert Emanuel, 22, and Gary Dolton, 19. The marathon men were confident of speedy recognition by the *Guinness Book of Records*: their log book was signed by nearly 1,000 passersby.

□

Among the world's most avid Scrabbloholics is actress Valerie Perrine, who was nominated for an Academy Award for her portrayal of Lenny Bruce's wife, Honey, in the film *Lenny*. Her agent, Richard Grant, at Rogers and Cowan, public relations, told me: "Valerie is indeed an avid Scrabble player, but interestingly enough, her playing, for the most part, takes place while she is working on a film. She finds it a superb way to relax. Her favorite opponent just happens to be Dustin Hoffman, with whome she played often during the filming of *Lenny*.

How well does she score, and does the former Las Vegas show girl have any special strategy? "She doesn't recall her best score for a single word or her best score for a game," Grant said, "but her game strategy is the obvious one of saving her numerically big letters for double- and triple-point squares. Valerie also happens to have an incredibly large vocabulary, which is obviously of great help to her game."

□

Did you know that Scrabble had been on the cover of *Time* magazine? Well, almost. The magazine carried a cover story in May 1969 on Russian-born novelist and poet, Vladimir Nabokov. Nabokov, it turns out, is a Scrabble buff, and behind his portrait on the magazine cover were easily recognizable Scrabble tiles—in Russian Cyrillic letters.

□

In 1953–54, when Scrabble was America's biggest craze, *Look* magazine called it "the new parlormania," and the game was extensively written up in all major magazines. *Time* magazine's sister publication, *Life*, ran a long feature on the invention of the game by Butts and on Brunot's so-called "quiet little business in the country," which was being swamped with unfillable Scrabble orders. At *Look* magazine they constructed a giant "Scrabble" board so that they could photograph Butts and Brunot looking like two midgets playing a game.

□

Butts can't remember his best-ever single-word score. His wife can remember hers: on October 27, 1956, Nina Butts scored a triple-triple with the word *quixotic*. For that she got 284 points—the highest score ever in the Butts household. Their best combined game score was 853, a total described by Butts as "a once in a lifetime thing."

□

Want to win a Scrabble bet? Wager with a know-it-all opponent that he cannot name a word that not only contains every vowel in the alphabet, but also contains the letter *Y* as a vowel. And not only that. This word uses them all in sequence. The word is *facetiously*. Another one is *abstemiously*.

A Sydney, Australia, Scrabble buff for 20 years spends her time constructing sentences from as many tiles as possible. The best effort so far for Mrs. J. D. Ramsbottom, according to the *Sydney Morning Herald*, is the following: "The zebras are bounding too anxiously alongside miles of quick flowing river water just to evade painted pea machinery."

That "painted pea" may sound a trifle weird, but the sentence does use all 100 letters in a game. Another Sydney Scrabble fan, Mr. V. Wasley, of Coff's Harbor, came up with the following: "However did pavid bodies find time to enjoy an exercise, using all tiles, making up queer words for a tale about a crazy thing?"

And that's the last word on that.

□

Nobody likes a Scrabble smart-ass. The following, though, is a classic "I told you so" Scrabble tale. Inventor Butts was playing a game with his elder brother, Allison. The word *zinc* was on the board, and Allison tried to make it *dezinc*. Both Butts and his wife, Nina, challenged the word, even though the brother had impressive credentials: he was a professor of metallurgy at Lehigh University.

"I told him there was absolutely no such word," Alfred Butts recalled. "It's in Webster's," Allison Butts smugly replied. "I put it there." Unbeknown to Alfred Butts, his brother had been approached by the editorial board at Webster's to adjudicate on metallurgical words for a revised edition. One of those words was *dezinc*.

"We had to let him have it," Alfred Butts said.

□

"Some people came looking for me at my place in the country," Alfred Butts said, recalling the early days. "A Chinese family lived next door, and they asked the husband if he knew where I lived. 'Oh, yes, he's the gambler, isn't he?' Because I'd invented a game, he thought I was a playboy," Butts said.

Actually, Butts has never played his game for money.

□

England's best-known royal entrepreneur, the duke of Bedford, once hosted a Scrabble tournament at Woburn Abbey—the palatial estate where he offended his fellow bluebloods by installing turnstiles in the castle walls and selling souvenirs to the tourists to pay death duties on his father's estate. Not only did the duke host the tournament—he won it. Years later I asked him for details. From his new home on the Quai d'Orléans in Paris, the duke of Bedford wrote: "I remember the time I won the competition. It was sponsored by whoever were the promoters of Scrabble in England at that time. There were a number of distinguished people there, but it was all so long ago that I cannot remember who they were."

He said his victory in the tournament was "complete and utter luçk," but that everybody imagined the competition was rigged. "It was really very embarrassing, but the whole thing was completely honest," he wrote. "I just happened to get two words that went from top to bottom and horizontally. It was naturally just pure chance." The duke said he hardly played Scrabble any more because he now lives in France, "and my French is so appalling that I cannot know any words of more than three or four letters so that my score is not good."

□

Although, as mentioned earlier, Leonard Bernstein does not have a thousand-dollar Scrabble set custom-made out of ivory, somebody somewhere has, or at least had, a set made in morocco leather and worth about $400. Jim Brunot recalls that the special order was commissioned in the early 1950s as a gimmick for a leatherware display at the Fifth Avenue store of W. & J. Sloane's. "They had at least one made up. Maybe more," he said. "I remember the board was leather-backed, and there was a special hand-tooled leather case. The price was incredible. It was more than $400, as I recall." It is not known whether or not the set was sold. All they know at Sloane's is that it isno longer in stock.

□

Anybody who owns one of the original Brunot Scrabble boards will have trouble if he or she tries to match up the sample game diagrams in the lid of the box with the scores mentioned. Add them up and see. The scores are wrong. What happened was that Brunot used one of Butts's old boards, which had a slightly different premium square distribution. "We goofed on that one," Brunot said.

□

At one stage when Butts was planning the game, the premiun squares included a "quadruple word square." It was located near the bottom right-hand corner of the board and was used as an incentive to spread the words when the starting star was not in the center but in the top left-hand corner of the board. The quadruple square was dropped when Butts moved the starting position back into the middle. "The other way just didn't work," he said.

□

Jim Brunot also played around with the design and even the size of the board. He once tried to make a Whopper Scrabble set. That didn't work either. "To keep the triple-word square pattern the same and to keep the premium squares more than seven tiles apart, you had to go to at least a board that measured 23 squares by 23 squares," Brunot said. "Then we found that to keep the luck and skill ration the same, we had to have nearly 300 tiles."

□

Alfred Butts played on the school chess team when he was in college, but quit because "it was no fun."

□

Lee Tiffany, president of the Scrabble® Crossword Game Players®, Inc., does not play Scrabble. "I'm not going to go home and do what I work at," he said. "I'm more analytical. I like the sport of analyzing score sheets and following a game through that way." But, says Tiffany, it's not important that he does not personally play the game. "I could sell great advertising for Kotex although I don't wear it," he said.

INDEX

213